Fearful Times; Living Faith

Fearful Times; Living Faith

Edited by
Robert Boak Slocum
and Martyn Percy

WIPF & STOCK · Eugene, Oregon

FEARFUL TIMES; LIVING FAITH

Wipf & Stock
An Imprint of Wipf and Stock Publishers
199 W. 8th Ave., Suite 3
Eugene, OR 97401

www.wipfandstock.com

PAPERBACK ISBN: 978-1-6667-3155-2
HARDCOVER ISBN: 978-1-6667-2420-2
EBOOK ISBN: 978-1-6667-2421-9

NOVEMBER 17, 2021

Unless otherwise stated, the New Revised Standard Version (NRSV) translation is used throughout this book.

Scripture quotations marked (GNT) are from the Good News Translation in Today's English Version- Second Edition Copyright © 1992 by American Bible Society. Used by Permission.

Scripture quotations marked HCSB are taken from the Holman Christian Standard Bible®, Used by Permission HCSB ©1999,2000,2002,2003,2009 Holman Bible Publishers. Holman Christian Standard Bible®, Holman CSB®, and HCSB® are federally registered trademarks of Holman Bible Publishers.

We dedicate this book to the frontline workers of these fearful times—healthcare providers, first responders, teachers, law enforcement, store clerks, and other essential workers, everyone whose work is service that keeps society going in these times.

RBS ⌇ MP

Contents

Acknowledgements

Special thanks to Victoria Slocum for help in the editing and preparation of this book. Thanks also to Jessica Oliver for assistance with communications for this project. Thanks to Sam Portaro, Sarah Cotes, Ellen Clark-King, Bob Hughes, Christina Rees, Alan Jones, Dan Joslyn-Siemiatkoski, and Debra Trakel for helpful suggestions.

Introduction

WE LIVE IN FEARFUL TIMES with many threats and horrors. We've seen a pandemic, systemic racism and violence, resurgent nationalism and tribalism, polarization and mutual suspicion, insurrection, environmental peril due to climate change, and on and on. There are unexpected things we can't predict or control. We can feel helpless. But these threats give impetus for reflection on what faith has to say in challenging times, in any time.

Where do we turn in real need? What makes a difference? What do we really believe? The current situation brings the reality of our connectedness with each other into sharp focus. What does our faith mean and what does it offer now for grace, comfort, and transformation? People need to hear it and the church needs to say it through witness and writings. Can we speak in Christ's name against dishonesty, cruelty, and neglect of the most needy and vulnerable in a time of crisis? The pandemic and other horrors provide the catalyst, the jumping-off point for theology that lives today and in the future, in fearful times and whatever comes next. To all appearances this may be the worst of times. But the best can come out of the worst. That's a truth for anyone who sees love in a cross.

Where do we turn when overwhelmed by threats and uncertainty? Austin Farrer (1904–1968) uses the image of a person deciding whether a plank makes a safe step. It's a judgment call, an interesting question, but the outcome can be existential if the plank doesn't hold. The question is no longer abstract when the person puts weight on the plank. If the plank holds, the question has an answer. The moment of decision forecloses an agnostic suspension of judgment. We may know God as we act in faith. Farrer states it's often in the moment of particular action that we discover whether we really believe something or not.[1] Where do you put your foot for the next step? It's a vital choice in a perilous dilemma, in fearful times.

As Christians, as people of faith, how do we find God alive in us and present in our turmoil? How may we discover ourselves already found by amazing grace? And how do we share that hope with others? What are the solid planks that uphold us? What empowers us to speak truth, call out lies, seek justice, and respect others? What beckons us forward with new questions, open hearts, a willingness to risk and discover? How can Christian faith help us bring the best out of the worst? How can we raise the cross? Can we rediscover our faith, our church, our lives in these times of crisis? Can we "sing to the Lord a new song?" Where do we start?

As we face unanticipated challenges and unexpected horrors, may we find a new shape of Christian belief, hope, and practice.

This volume presents a variety of perspectives and answers for questions of fearful times and living faith (submitted from summer 2020 to spring 2021). Hear them all.

ROBERT BOAK SLOCUM

1. Farrer, "The Rational Grounds for Belief in God," 7; Slocum, *Light in a Burning-Glass*, 7.

Living Faith in Fearful Times

Four Stories

ROBERT BOAK SLOCUM

IN FEARFUL TIMES WE do well to draw on the best that faith provides for hope, guidance, and strength. We stand with others, a "cloud of witnesses" speaking in love to every threat and occasion. This chapter is a "gallery" of witnesses and scenes, glimpses of God with us and visible in the lives of people who faced their own fearful times with living faith—in times of plague, murder, war, racist violence, and martyrdom.

Bells for the Dying, the Dead, and the Living

John Donne (1572–1631), poet, Anglican priest, and Dean of St Paul's, London, lived in a time of bubonic plague and epidemic. In 1623 he found himself stricken with fever and in grave danger. Izaac Walton states that when Donne was fifty-four "a dangerous sicknesse seised him, which turned to a spotted Feaver, and ended in a Cough, that inclined him to a Consumption," and "this sicknesse brought him to the gates of death."[1] Donne's illness was known as "spotted fever" or "relapsing fever," and it was

---

1. Walton, "Life and Death," xxxiii.

epidemic in London. It is now known as typhus.[2] John Booty notes it was typical for patients with this condition to be mentally alert but physically weak as the disease ran its course.[3]

Donne wrote and edited his *Devotions upon Emergent Occasions* during this precarious time of illness and convalescence. Edmund Gosse states "nowhere in the whole of Donne's writings do we obtain quite so personal an impression of him as in these strange notes concerning the progress of his illness in the winter of 1623." Gosse laments that at one point "the autobiographical value of these confessions" was overlooked because they were "buried in masses of scholastic divinity" that Donne wrote. But when the autobiographical notes about his illness and recovery were "removed from these dull wrappings," it was possible to "be struck with their acute observation, their subtle psychological freshness."[4]

Donne was deeply affected by the sound of bells ringing for the dying and the dead from the "church adjoining" as he faced mortality in the Deanery of St. Paul's. Clara Lander notes that "the incessant ringing of bells" would have surrounded Donne in his illness because "as the typhus epidemic reached its peak, the bells of London tolled continually for the dead and dying." She urges "the atmosphere in Devotions XVI, XVII and XVIII seems possessed with bells, and suggests the impact they must have had on the consciousness, as well as the conscience, of every citizen of London, particularly those already stricken."[5]

Donne struggled with insomnia and was "extremely annoyed by the Cathedral bells."[6] Donne described himself as a "prisoner" in his sick bed "so near to that (2021) steeple that never ceases, no more than the harmony of the spheres, but is more heard." Those bells moved him because they rang for others: "Here the bells can scarce solemnize the funeral of any person, but that I knew him, or knew that he was my neighbor: we dwelt in houses near to one another before, but now he is gone into that house into which I must follow him."[7]

---

2. Lander, "Per Fretum Febris," 264. She notes that in London in 1624 "the weekly toll rose at times to over five hundred typhus deaths."

3. Booty, "Introduction: A Brief Life," 10–44.

4. Gosse, *Life and Letters of John Donne*, 186.

5. Lander, "Per Fretum Febris," 36–37.

6. Gosse, *Life and Letters of John Donne*, 185.

7. Donne, "Devotion XVI," 267.

The insistent bells recalled Donne to his deep connectedness with others through the church. He says the baptism of a child "concerns me" because "that child is thereby connected to that body which is my head too, and ingrafted into that body whereof I am a member." Likewise, when the church buries a person, "that action concerns me: all mankind is of one author, and is one volume." We share hope for the future when God's "hand shall bind up all our scattered leaves again for that library where every book shall lie open to one another." Donne states the bell that summons us to divine union with God "calls us all," and especially Donne who was "brought so near the door by this sickness." This bell calls each of us and it calls us together. No one is "an island."[8] In God we are one with another. In a time of plague and epidemic, bells for the dead and dying reminded Donne of life for all in divine union together.

Prayers for a Murderer

In the summer of 1887 Thérèse Martin (1873–97), a devout fourteen-year-old in Lisieux, France, learned that Henri Pranzini was convicted of the murder of two women and a twelve-year-old girl in Paris. He was sentenced to death. Pranzini proclaimed his innocence when arrested and at trial, but there was overwhelming evidence of his guilt. The triple murder was notorious, and in the French papers "there was much talk about the viciousness of the crime, the depravity of the criminal, and the rightness of the execution."[9] Thérèse, later known as Thérèse of Lisieux, recalled in her autobiography *Story of a Soul* that "everything pointed to the fact that he would die impenitent. I wanted at all costs to prevent him from falling into hell, and to attain my purpose I employed every means imaginable."[10] Patricia O'Connor notes "as the newspapers fed the French public's appetite for brutal details, Thérèse prayed."[11] She begged for grace and sought the conversion of "the guilty man." She described him as her "first child," and asked in prayer for a sign of his repentance. She found it when she read a newspaper account that Pranzini on the scaffold reverenced a crucifix before his death. Thérèse rejoiced at the news.[12] She prayed for many others.

8. Donne, "Devotion XVII," 271–72.

9. Schmidt, *Everything Is Grace*, 138.

10. Thérèse of Lisieux, *Story of a Soul*, 99.

11. O'Connor, *In Search of Thérèse*, 102.

12. Thérèse of Lisieux, *Story of a Soul*, 100.

Thérèse had little in common with Pranzini beyond shared humanity. She didn't know him. He was said to be a foreigner. He committed horrible crimes and lied about it. He showed no remorse and gave no sign of a change of heart until the very last. He was not deserving of her attention in any conventional sense. But Thérèse hoped her prayers would help him know forgiveness and salvation in Christ. She was audacious enough to accept a big challenge and hope for something more. She prayed for the guilty man. She knew he was not beyond God's love or human compassion in a horrible situation of his own making.

Christmas in No Man's Land[13]

As Christmas drew near in 1914, the warring German and allied armies were stalemated. They were entrenched on the 475 miles of the western front of Europe from the North Sea to the Swiss border. It was the first Christmas of the first World War. Conditions were miserable, icy, and muddy. Cold water was in the trenches, at times up to the knees. The opposing trenches were in shouting distance of each other, sometimes within fifty yards. The lines were separated by entanglements of barbed wire and a narrow "no man's land" that was a killing field.

But the soldiers along the lines made their own truce. They quit killing each other for Christmas. The initiative came from the soldiers in the trenches, not generals or national leaders. There is no telling exactly where the Christmas truce first began, but a time of peace came in many places in different ways along the lines. Hundreds of truces were arranged on Christmas morning "all along the Western Front."[14] The truces began differently so there are many accounts. The Germans frequently took the initiative, sometimes with messages on sign boards in broken English for the other side: "YOU NO FIGHT, WE NO FIGHT." The Germans placed small Christmas trees with burning candles at the front of the parapets of their trenches.

On Christmas Eve at Armentières, Albert Moren of the British 2nd Queen's Regiment recalled "It was a beautiful moonlit night, frost on the ground, white almost everywhere." He remembered "those lights" from the

---

13. This section drawn in part from Slocum, "Christmas Trees and Chocolate Cake," np.

14. Boyle, *Peace on Earth*, 69.

German side, "And then they sang 'Silent Night'—'*Stille Nacht*." He said "I shall never forget it. It was one of the highlights of my life."[15]

At Houplines the Second Royal Welch Fusiliers put up a sign board message for the Germans: "A MERRY CHRISTMAS." Soon afterwards representatives from both sides met between the lines and shook hands, and then "the trenches emptied and men on both sides began running toward each other" to share the truce.[16]

At Ploegsteert Wood the singing of carols became almost antiphonal. The Germans sang "*Stille Nacht*," and clapped when the London Rifles sang "The First Nowell." When the British started "O Come All Ye Faithful," the Germans joined in with "*Adeste Fidelis*," the Latin words for the same carol.[17] Early on Christmas morning Edward Roe in the East Lancashire trenches was amazed to discover the rumors of a truce were not a joke. "And there they were, sure enough," he later recalled, "British and German warriors in No Man's Land, talking to each other and exchanging souvenirs. There is a Christ after all."[18]

Corporal John Ferguson of the Seaforth Highlanders north of Ploegsteert Wood also recalled an amazing Christmas scene: "what a sight—little groups of Germans and British extending almost the length of our front!" It was a startling change. "Here we were laughing and chatting to men whom only a few hours before we were trying to kill!"[19]

After the truce began, the soldiers met in the middle of the killing field. They were friendly. They exchanged food, drink, tobacco, and personal items such as photographs, buttons, and badges. They played soccer. Boyle notes "if the Germans seem to have taken the lead in most, though not all, cases of the original truce, it was clearly the British who led the way when it came to football."[20] The soldiers sang carols and made toasts. They chased a hare together. They recovered and buried the dead, even with a joint funeral service for the fallen on both sides. In some places the truce was just for a day, but in other places the truce lasted past Christmas. Murphy

15. Weintraub, *Silent Night*, 44.

16. Weintraub, *Silent Night*, 81–82.

17. Boyle, *Peace on Earth*, 40; Murphy, *Truce*, 58–59.

18. Boyle, *Peace on Earth*, 43.

19. Weintraub, *Silent Night*, 79–80.

20. Boyle, *Peace on Earth*, 61–62.

notes "some areas held on to their truces for as long as possible" and that in Ploegsteert Wood "little hard fighting took place until early spring."[21]

The allied troops had been exposed to propaganda that described the German soldiers as barbarians. But they found their enemies to be very much like themselves. Boyle states that "the description of the two sides running towards each other in No Man's Land implies more than a reluctant handshake; it implies a sudden thrilling revelation of how much they had in common."[22] It was a Christmas surprise.

Tear Gas and Freedom[23]

Jonathan Daniels (1939–65) was preparing for ordination at the Episcopal Theological School (ETS) in Cambridge, Massachusetts, in 1965 when he went to Alabama to join a nonviolent march for civil rights from Selma to the state capitol in Montgomery. He answered Martin Luther King Jr.'s call for religious leaders in the United States to join this march after state and local law enforcement officers violently broke up an earlier march from Selma to Montgomery on "Bloody Sunday," March 7, 1965, at the Edmund Pettus Bridge in Selma.

At first Jonathan was reluctant to leave seminary during an academic term to join the struggle for civil rights in Alabama. The idea seemed "impractical." He went to Evening Prayer at his seminary as he considered his decision. He recalled singing the Magnificat "with the special love and reverence I have always felt for Mary's glad song." As the hymn continued, Jonathan was "peculiarly alert, suddenly straining toward the decisive, luminous, spirit-filled 'moment,' . . . Then it came. 'He hath put down the mighty from their seat, and hath exalted the humble and meek. He hath filled the hungry with good things.'" In that moment Jonathan knew he had to go to Selma.[24]

Jonathan continued to work for civil rights in Selma under the sponsorship of the Episcopal Society for Cultural and Racial Unity (ESCRU).

---

21. Murphy, *Truce*, 87.

22. Boyle, *Peace on Earth*, 93.

23. This section originally appeared in Slocum, "Jonathan Daniels." Copyright 2020, The Historical Society of the Episcopal Church (www.hsec.us).

24. Eagles, *Outside Agitator*, 27; Schneider, *American Martyr*, 105; See Luke 1:46–55. Mary was pregnant with Jesus and visiting her kinswoman Elizabeth who was pregnant with John, later known as John the Baptist.

His ministry for civil rights and social justice in Alabama had many expressions, as he described: "Sometimes we take to the streets, sometimes we yawn through interminable meetings. . . . Sometimes we confront the posse, and sometimes we hold a child."[25] Alabama was a dangerous place during the civil rights movement of the 1960s. Demonstrators and civil rights activists faced extreme and violent resentment from local opponents of desegregation. Whites from outside Alabama who resisted segregation were considered "outside agitators."

Jonathan was amazed by the freedom he discovered through faith when facing severe challenges. He found the freedom to give himself. He even discovered his freedom for a change of heart. He described how he was tempted to violence by the racism and brutality around him. "At first," he wrote to Molly D. Thoron, "I think I should gladly have procured a high-powered rifle and taken to the woods—to fight the battle as the Klansmen do." He "was very, very angry: with white people."[26]

But Jonathan's perspective began to change when he was tear-gassed while leading a voter registration march on April 7, 1965, in Camden, Alabama. The population of that county was about 80 percent black, but no Blacks were registered to vote there at the beginning of 1965. Jonathan and other activists were gassed during an attempted march in Camden. This was a turning point for Jonathan.[27] In Camden he saw the men coming at him "were themselves not free" but "*they didn't know what else to do.*" Instead of anger, he found himself "feeling a kind of grim affection for them."[28]

Jonathan said he previously had "realized that as a Christian, as a 'soldier of the Cross,' I was totally free—at least free to give my life, if that had to be, with joy and thankfulness and eagerness for the Kingdom no longer hidden from my blind eyes." There was nothing to fear anywhere "in all of Creation" but his own blindness. He said "last week in Camden I began to discover a new freedom in the Cross: freedom to love the enemy. And in that freedom, the freedom (without hypocrisy) to will and to try to set him free."[29]

Jonathan's path of faith continued from Camden to Haynesville, Alabama, where he sacrificed his life on August 20, 1965, to save a Black civil

---

25. Daniels, "Burning Bush," 91.

26. Schneider, *American Martyr*, 72–73.

27. Eagles, *Outside Agitator*, 62–64.

28. Schneider, *American Martyr*, 73.

29. Schneider, *American Martyr*, 73.

rights worker from murder. When confronted by an armed challenger he pushed Ruby Sales out of danger and was shot to death.

Jonathan shared his life and freedom gladly. He once told a mass (2019) meeting in a rural Alabama church that "his freedom depended on their freedom."[30] By faith he was freed from fear. Jonathan wrote in a seminary paper that he lost fear in Alabama "when I began to know in my bones and sinews that I had truly been baptized into the Lord's death and Resurrection, that in the only sense that really matters I am already (2014) dead, and my life is hid with Christ in God."[31] The presence of God in Jonathan's life set him free to love, to serve, to risk, and to sacrifice. Shortly after the march to Montgomery he wrote: "I have the haunting feeling again and again that I am flying with the mightiest Wind in the world at my back."[32] In fearful times Jonathan discovered freedom, inspiration, and living faith.

30. Eagles, *Outside Agitator*, 138.

31. Daniels, "June 22, 1965," in Schneider, *American Martyr*, 110.

32. Schneider, *American Martyr*, 70.

2

The Fears of Today
for the Hope of Tomorrow[1]

Gulnar (Guli) Francis-Dehqani

A Personal Backdrop

I STARTED LIFE IN Iran where I was born and grew up in the city of Isfahan. My father was a Muslim convert and my mother, the daughter and granddaughter of missionaries, herself born and raised in Iran. I lived an unusual life between and betwixt the worlds of Islam and Christianity, Persian and English, East and West. At home, life focused around the church with its mixture of converts, second-generation Persian Christians, missionaries and other foreigners working in Iran. This was my normal. It was all I knew and for the most part my two worlds coexisted peaceably with some occasional overlap. Everything changed as the Islamic Revolution of 1979 began to unfold. At school I was ostracized by friends and teachers; at home, the church was coming under increasing pressure. Institutions were confiscated or closed, church offices and the bishop's house were ransacked, financial assets were frozen, one of the clergy was murdered in his study,

---

1. This chapter is an abridged version of a talk I first gave at the Diocese of Lichfield Clergy Conference in April 2018.

my father (who was bishop) was briefly imprisoned before an attack on his life in which my mother was injured.[2]

For our family, events culminated with the murder of my brother, Bahram, aged twenty-four.[3] My father was out of the country, for meetings at the time and no one was ever brought to justice. Bahram was targeted because of his association with the church, because he was his father's son. After his funeral, knowing it was unsafe for my father to return, my mother and sister and I joined him in England, assuming we'd be back home within the year. That was not to be and, having arrived as a refugee aged fourteen, I remain in the United Kingdom forty-one years later, a fully-fledged British citizen.

Identity

For Anglicans in Iran our context was a missionary church developing its own identity as an authentically Persian community within an environment where national identity was overwhelmingly regarded as coterminous with religious identity. In the West, faith is generally regarded as a personal matter whereas in the East it is deeply rooted in the perception of one's culture, racial ties, and heritage; faith strikes at the core of one's identity. In Iran, to be Persian was (and is) to be Muslim, specifically Shi'a Muslim. To *not* be Muslim was regarded as a kind of betrayal of your nationality, raising questions about your identity, who you were and how you fitted in. Not surprisingly, questions around identity and belonging have been significant for me throughout my life. For the church in Iran it was about how we could be both Christian *and* Persian. For me personally, there's been a quest to discover who I am and how I fit in.

Farifteh Robb (a Persian Christian immigrant to Britain like me) expresses accurately a feeling I remember well. *I longed to slot neatly and inconspicuously into a single culture but instead I felt like an apologetic European when among Persians, and an apologetic foreigner when mixing with Westerners.*[4] In other words, always a stranger and interloper; living with

2. For more on the impact of the Revolution on the Anglican Church in Iran see Dehqani-Tafti, *Hard Awakening*.

3. Bahram's car was ambushed on his way back from work on May 6, 1980. He was shot in the head and died instantly. For further details and reflections see Dehqani-Tafti, *Unfolding Design*, 208–13.

4. Robb, *In the Shadow of the Shahs*, 54 (I have adapted her words slightly).

the ever-present anxiety of never quite fitting in. The challenge has been to not get stuck in that place which is neither one thing nor another—to not sit on the boundaries, wallowing in self-pity as an outsider. But to be more creative, transforming my experience of the margins from that which defines me negatively, into something positive and meaningful.

I've explored how to find a sense of belonging and rootedness, an authentic voice which encompasses the full extent of my particular life experience and is expansive enough to be inclusive, enabling me to connect well with others (many of whom also feel on the margins for all kinds of reasons). This journey into a fuller self-discovery has been intrinsically bound up with the idea of hope—moving from self-doubt and anxiety towards self-acceptance and sanguinity. It's been about discovering who I am, not to locate myself in opposition to others, but to rejoice in my uniqueness and find a way of joining in fully, participating and contributing to the diversity which itself is a symbol of hope and inclusivity. In the words of Farifteh Robb again: "It is this reconciliation that has bestowed upon me the unexpected gift of abundant grace."[5]

Forgiveness

In the months and years after we left Iran, I witnessed my parents struggle, not only with the loss of their only son and the reality of exile, but with some central Christian themes. In particular, forgiveness and how it relates to hope. Even as I was grieving myself, I watched them traverse the painful path towards forgiving those who murdered their son. Through my teens I observed them adjust with graciousness to life in exile, and the apparent disintegration of all they had worked for in Iran. Slowly I began to realize they were demonstrating hope when all seemed lost.

I have a vivid recollection of hearing my father preach, while we were still in Iran but after the troubles had started. I must have been twelve or thirteen. He spoke of having preached about forgiveness for years but only now realising the words had been largely theoretical. He was feeling the burden of having to live the reality. It was easy to talk about forgiveness when it didn't cost very much. But now he could sense the time was coming to practice what he purported to believe. Forgiveness is a messy process; painful and costly. The desire to embrace it, the commitment to try to practice it may be instantaneous but the journey towards it is slow and

5. Robb, *In the Shadow of the Shahs*, 11.

meandering. Forgiveness is complex. There's no doubt it has at times been misused and perhaps even cheapened and abused by the church. This is not the place to explore it fully but we must be cautious in the language we use and never impose the idea on those who are suffering. That said, forgiveness remains a central Christian theme. It's a theme we can't avoid but must grapple with; and one that ties in with the themes of fear and hope.

The following prayer was written by my father after Bahram was killed. In Cyprus at the time, he dictated the words to my mother over the telephone. It was read, in its original Persian, at Bahram's funeral.[6]

> *O God, we remember not only Bahram but his murderers.*
> *Not because they killed him in the prime of his youth and made our hearts*
> *bleed and our tears flow;*
> *Not because with this savage act they have brought further disgrace on the*
> *name of our country among the civilized nations of the world;*
> *But because through their crime we now follow more closely your footsteps*
> *in the way of sacrifice.*
> *The terrible fire of this calamity burns up all selfishness and possessiveness*
> *in us.*
> *Its flame reveals the depth of depravity, meanness and suspicion, the di-*
> *mension of hatred and the measure of sinfulness in human nature;*
> *It makes obvious as never before our need to trust in your love as shown in*
> *the cross of Jesus and his resurrection,*
> *Love that makes us free from all hatred towards our persecutors;*
> *Love which brings patience, forbearance, courage, loyalty, humility, gener-*
> *osity and greatness of heart;*
> *Love which more than ever deepens our trust in God's final victory and his*
> *eternal designs for the Church and for the world;*
> *Love which teaches us how to prepare ourselves to face our own day of*
> *death.*
> *O God,*
> *Bahram's blood has multiplied the fruit of the Spirit in the soil of our souls:*
> *so when his murderers stand before you on the Day of Judgment,*
> *remember the fruit of the Spirit by which they have enriched our lives,*
> *and forgive.*

Though the word hope is never used, the prayer is infused with a hopeful spirit. It defines forgiveness as that which allows us to trust more completely, freeing us from hatred, enabling us to love, releasing us from

---

6. This is the English translation that has become known as the forgiveness prayer. It can be found in Appleton, *Oxford Book of Prayer*, 135. I have modified the language to make it more contemporary.

anxiety about our own death. I wish I'd quizzed my father more but it seems to me his words are brimming with hope-filled sentiments. He seemed to be saying *you need pain and suffering to fully comprehend the meaning of hope, and the gateway between the two is forgiveness.* Through pain we can understand more fully how to trust, thereby catching a vivid glimpse of hope. Hope is nothing if it does not exist when all seems hopeless. You have to experience fear, anxiety, pain, hopelessness, to truly know what hope is. Indeed, "perhaps hopelessness is the very soil that nourishes human hope."[7] We have to inhabit the fear and suffering of Good Friday and dwell with it, if we are to taste the hope and joy of Easter resurrection.

Facing our Fears

Hope is not some sentimental feeling of happiness or wishful thinking. It's not a mood but a virtue, a strength of character. And virtues don't come out of nothing but have to be rehearsed: "practices build virtues."[8] Saint Paul writes: "Meanwhile, these three remain, faith, hope and love."[9] Three Christian virtues that we must *practice;* and hope is, perhaps, the least well-exercised. We seem instinctively to understand that love and faith must be practiced even when we may not feel like it. We cannot only love when the mood takes us; faith must be nourished daily. That is equally true of hope though we don't always recognise it.

The prophet Ezekiel was amongst the exiles in Babylon around 600 BCE. During twenty-five years of exile he experienced every kind of anguish imaginable and yet as he considered his situation and the future of Israel, he was far from despondent. In 47:1, Ezekiel sees a trickle of water flowing out from below the entrance to the temple. A tiny sign of life that would have been easy to miss but Ezekiel, practiced in the art of hope, notices and follows it. The paltry trickle gradually grows, becoming first a stream and eventually a mighty river, transforming the landscape, producing fertile soil and fruitfulness on every side. His hope-filled eyes spot new life wherever the river flows. Like Ezekiel we are called to be people of hope, those who discern the tiniest hints of it and who foster and nourish it. Signs

---

7. Attributed to Vaclav Havel. See, for example, http://www.notable-quotes.com/h/havel_vaclav.html

8. Welby, *Reimagining Britain*, 3.

9. 1 Cor 13:13.

of God's presence are all around; we need only look, notice and water the seeds.

So, what prevents us from seeing and noticing, from living as people of hope? Worry, anxiety, and fear—these are enemies of hope. They distort our vision, paralyze, and prevent us from practicing hope. But before we can banish or let go of them, we must address them—look them in the eye, as it were. And not just name them but properly voice our anguish and lament, grieving for what we have lost, for the future that might have been. And of course there is good precedent for this: the Lamentations of Jeremiah, the story of Job, and many of the Psalms, for example. They give voice, communally and individually, to our anger, frustration, fear, and grief, all of which is held and contained by God—just like a mother holds and comforts her distraught child even when she can't make things better or offer any answers. Sometimes we may encounter only silence—perhaps a sign of the anguish at the heart of God; God's own sorrow and pain, God's own lament. Kuang-hsun Ting reminds us that the Bible is not a blue print with all the answers but includes within itself many silences—blank spaces we are invited to fill in. These are question marks that challenge us to find signs of hope, answers appropriate for the spirit of our time.[10]

Hurt and pain, grief and suffering are not good in themselves; but psychologists tell us if we face reality, acknowledge our emotions, express rage and fury, we have a better chance of coming through. Not unscathed, of course, for scars remain just as they did with the risen Christ. But having confronted our fears and dwelt in the darkness, we are better placed to begin the process of healing and recognize signs of hope and resurrection. We might take this still one step further and say that to journey through lament to hope, we must look for some kind of meaning, a flicker of light in the darkness. Ezekiel recognized the destruction of the temple as God's judgement on the people. By finding meaning in his experience, he reshaped what might have been complete despondency into the possibility of hope.

As the revolution was gathering storm in Iran, my father spoke these words which I still have on a poster on my study wall: "The way of the cross has suddenly become so meaningful that we have willingly walked in it with our Lord near us. Our numbers have become smaller, our earthly supports have gone, but we are learning the meaning of faith in a new and deeper way." Things were not turning out as my father wanted or imagined. Here, he mourns the past, acknowledges present reality, and finds meaning

10. Ting, "Chinese Example," 431–33.

therein. The revolution brought the opportunity for a closer walk with God, a whole new way of experiencing the cross; it offered the possibility of practicing that fragile Christian virtue of hope.

Kingdom Values

For Christians, one of our challenges is to avoid being seduced by worldly ideas about success, influence and relevance. All you have to do is look at the Beatitudes or indeed the cross to know that God's wisdom is utter foolishness to the world. The church has never been at its best when it's been large or powerful. Consider the Crusades, Western imperialism which saw Christianity as one arm of a wider cultural and military expansion. Think today of the large prosperity churches, especially in the United States with their message of wealth and success. These are distortions of our faith and of the example we have in the person of Jesus who offered a whole new vision of authority by kneeling at his disciples' feet to wash their feet, radically subverting worldly values.

The Church of England is currently awash with programs and strategies for growth—a drive to increase numbers and prevent our demise. There's nothing wrong with this and certainly we are called to be missional. But there are pitfalls and dangers. Chiefly, if we are driven by fear and anxiety we will never succeed. So let us liberate ourselves from fear and anxiety, lament the past, release it and be free of it. Let us find meaning in present reality and discover hope for the future.

Perhaps the days when the church was a big fish are over for a reason. In Iran, the work the church did through educational and medical institutions was foundational and structures were in place to support this ministry. Once dismantled forcibly, the church had to find meaning in the new reality. The loss of things once valuable and important enabled the church to discern God speaking in new ways, beckoning the faithful to a deeper level of trust. Is it possible that something like this is going on in Britain? What might God be saying in this new era? What might we being asked to lay down alongside the reduction of influence, smaller congregations, and loss of status? Are we clinging on for fear and anxiety; or do we hear the still small voice calling us to a new future that will look different and demand different things of us. In the spirit of Brother Lawrence, perhaps it is time to give up great ambitions and learn instead to do little things to the glory of God.[11] Perhaps we need to embrace our place on the margins and find an authentic voice that speaks both with confidence and generosity. Tom Wright reminds us that the mission of the church is not *building* the kingdom (that's God's work) but building *for* the kingdom.[12] Let's not confuse our calling to be salt in the world, to make Christ known through word and deed, with how big we are, how seriously we're taken, or how much influence we have.

My father used to say the church in Iran was like the pearl of great price—small and precious, treasured by God. What are the small treasures we have in the Church of England that are precious to God and how may we cherish them? To all intents and purposes, everything the missionaries worked for in Iran, all that my parents and many others gave their lives for (some quite literally) has been wasted. In worldly terms the experiment failed. And yet . . . this tiny persecuted community, with its faithful remnant, shines as a beacon of hope, enduring against all odds. Its very existence is miraculous; who knows how God is at work and what the future holds?

Hope lives on in faithfulness; in offering what we can, joyfully, free of fear and anxiety. This is not an excuse to sit back and do nothing but an assurance that God will work through our efforts as God sees fit and not as we may imagine.

---

11. Adam, *Aiden, Bede, Cuthbert,* 6–7.

12. Wright, *Surprised by Hope,* 218–19.

3

White Supremacy, Among the Giant Triplets

Bill Wylie-Kellermann

When the Roman Emperor Constantine "converted" to Christianity in the fourth century CE, or more aptly when he successfully converted the church to empire, a reinterpretation of Scripture was necessary.[1] New Testament terms related to political forces (rulers of this age, thrones, dominions, authorities, principalities, and powers) almost suddenly came to be read solely as spirits disconnected from corporate, institutional, structural, indeed imperial realities. Their essential criticism was gutted.[2] Constantine was off the hook. None of these refer to you, my Lord. And for centuries the church was denied or otherwise forewent access to an entire language of social and political critique.

Some things cannot even be seen or recognized without being named. Here, an entire biblical lexicon of names was relegated to the shelf. For much of the last century it was argued that the New Testament offered only an individual or personal ethic. To construct a social ethic, one needed to consult the prophets or the Hebrew Bible. And so it was that the rise of liberation theologies turned firstly to the exodus narratives.

---

1. Portions of this essay are adapted from an article, Wylie-Kellermann, "Not Against Flesh and Blood," 14–18.

2. "The church soon found itself the darling of Constantine. Called on to legitimate the empire, the church abandoned much of its social critique. The Powers were soon divorced from political affairs and made airy spirits who preyed only on individuals. The state was thus freed of one of the most powerful brakes against idolatry." Wink, *Naming the Powers*, 113.

It took various historical crises to pull the principalities lexicon from the shelf and refill its terms with meaning. In Europe the rise of fascism in Nazi Germany made these words light up for Christians engaged in resistance, both ecclesial and civil. In the United States it took the anti-war resistance to the militarized state, on the one hand, and the African American freedom struggle on the other, to bring this language back onto the map of Christian social ethics. In 1967, when Martin Luther King, Jr. identified the "giant triplets" of racism, militarism, and extreme materialism, he was naming both a mock trinity, unholy and blasphemous, but also putting his finger on the reigning principalities in the United States, comingled in a system of domination.

At present a question hangs in the balance. Will a new generation of Christians in the United States actively engaging those same triplets, along with a further set of forces (armed white supremacy, militarized policing, official fascism, and climate catastrophe/environmental injustice), find this biblical terminology useful and illuminating? I am beginning to hope so.

In my own twenties, I met William Stringfellow (1928–1985), a "lay theologian," as he was called, or an "organic" one we might say. From the vantage of the freedom struggle and the anti-war movement, he was among the first in the United States, and I'm including here academics, biblical scholars, and certified theologians, to reground the principalities and powers in common reality. In 1964, he'd published a book, *Free in Obedience*, which named them as institutions, ideologies, and images.[3] He was just beginning to categorize what would become a detailed and practically endless listing. Think: nation and state, corporations, the law, capitalism, Marxism, neoliberalism, patriarchy, sports, science, career, money, technology, family, yes, white supremacy, even unions, movements, and churches, no less. He found the powers to be legion in both name and number.

I read that book in preparation for him speaking at my college. He sat to talk, frail from a yet-undiagnosed illness. But he spoke with fire in his eyes about the "power" of racism. The Black students, who said they'd never heard a white man talk like this, besieged him after with questions.

Later I learned that he'd begun seriously thinking on the principalities while doing street law in East Harlem. He'd gone to work there after graduating in 1956 from Harvard Law School. Poised for a lucrative practice, he was to all appearances making a bad career move. But from the people of his neighborhood he heard tell of the powers, particularly in the way they

3. Stringfellow, *Free in Obedience*, 53–59.

spoke of The Man, or the police, or the welfare bureaucracy, liberal philanthropy, absentee landlords, the mafia—as if they were predatory creatures occupying the neighborhood and arrayed against Black and Puerto Rican folk. (Here in Detroit, Rev. Mama Sandra Simmons just shorthands them as "monsters.") All ring a biblical bell: Our struggle is not with enemies of flesh and blood, but against the rulers, the authorities, against the worldly powers of this present darkness, against the spiritual forces of evil in high places. So began Stringfellow's work of unpacking and regrounding the powers.[4]

Stringfellow, in turn, became an elder and mentor to me in the ways and the wiles of the principalities.

From early on, he'd been attentive to the creation hymn in the first chapter of Colossians that proclaims them good and necessary for human life in society. In such terms, they have a life and integrity of their own, separate or separated from human beings. They are accountable to God in judgment for their vocation, their calling, their purpose to serve life and creation. And like human beings, they are subject to the fall, prone to confusion, distortion, and corruption. Even inversion. Where they are called to praise God and serve human life in creation, they end up presuming to take the place of God, and dehumanizing or enslaving human beings. They are become demonic.

White supremacy, though it has ancient and even biblical analogues, is a "modern" principality. Its inception coincides with European capital expansion and "scientific enlightenment." The latter not only desanctified and disenchanted the world, but sought to "objectively" categorize all of life into biological kingdoms, phylums, and classes—including, by extension, human beings according to race. The "savage races" had been discovered. This was necessary and convenient for the expansion project, the taking of land and the forcible extracting of human labor.

For our purposes here, white supremacy remains an exemplar in understanding the principalities. Subject to the fall, the powers suffer the effects of idolatry. Abetted by human beings they seek to supplant God, the Spirit of Life. They are idols, every one. Full blown, they are anti-Christ, which is to say anti-human. Their work is to capture and dehumanize. Whiteness itself becomes such an idol.

---

4. See Stringfellow, *Ethic for Christians*.

At the First Conference on Religion and Race in 1963, Stringfellow spoke controversially not only about the conference itself but in naming racism as a power:

> Or, to put it a bit differently, racism is not an evil in human hearts or minds, racism is a principality, a demonic power, a representative image, an embodiment of death, over which human beings have little or no control, but which works its awful influence over their lives. This is the power with which Jesus Christ was confronted and which, at great and sufficient cost, he overcame.[5]

A modern principality encountered and engaged by Jesus Christ? Indeed. By power of the cross (Col 2:15)? or resurrection (1 Cor 15:25)? There is fruit for theological and political reflection here.

Walter Wink, the activist theologian and biblical scholar who wrote a magisterial trilogy on the powers, following Stringfellow's lead, posited an ethical formula: the principalities must be named, unmasked, and engaged (by which he titled the three volumes of his work).[6]

How to engage white supremacy? Is there a way to withdraw the projection? The alienation of false worship? The New Testament writings do offer a multiplicitous view of powerly "redemption." They claim in the end, the principalities are unable to separate us from the love of God (Rom 8:38–39), can, in baptism, be "died to" and so be freed from (Col 2:20), can be addressed and even evangelized, called back to their authentic vocations (Eph 3:10), be met in nonviolent combat of the spirit (Eph 6:10–17), be laid bare, made a spectacle, and disarmed (Col 2:15), be dethroned, neutralized, and put under subjection (1 Cor 15:25–26; Eph 1:20), and be found subject to mortality, doomed (or graced even) to pass away (1 Cor 2:6–8).

What can this mean in our present moment for white supremacy? What could possibly be meant by redemption? Whiteness is not a culture as such, but ersatz, a mess of pottage from the beginning. It seems from its very foundation to be designed to dominate and destroy bodies, communities, and the creatures of Earth. What if white supremacy is simply among those powers doomed to pass away, and soon? What if it is the moment (even late) for this power to die, and for white people to die to it? Die out from under it? Even if doing so feels like being thrown to the ground in convulsions.

---

5. Stringfellow, "Care Enough to Weep."

6. Wink, *Naming the Powers*; Wink, *Unmasking the Powers*; Wink, *Engaging the Powers*.

We are in a time of deep historical conflict that marks a dangerous and unsettling moment, and which also holds the possibility of real transformation. In the United States a young, lifegiving movement has risen up to challenge white supremacy and summon a massive cultural shift. It confronts racism in its blunt and most visible violence: police brutality and killings. Little wonder the powers squeal and rage in backlash against it. They fight for survival and make that their sole and desperate purpose.

White supremacy as a principality is in systemic collusion with other powers. It has insinuated itself in law and policy, in the judicial system and mass incarceration, in the algorithms of data extraction, in systems of access to education, housing, food, and water. It's embedded in the mapping of social and geographic reality. And it has a spiritual grip.

One of Walter Wink's biblical insights was just this, that the powers have an interiority, an invisible aspect, a spiritual dimension that must be named for them to be seen and recognized. It is the genius of their seduction and grasp.[7] Remember, the legal apparatus of American apartheid, Jim Crow legislation, was repealed, judicially overridden, and legally dismantled. But because white supremacy has this spiritual dimension and capacity; it rises up and reconfigures itself in ever new and more guileful forms—even as chattel slavery itself had into Jim Crow.

To disentangle racism from our institutions and from ourselves, requires not just deconstruction, but exorcism if you will. Or nonviolent weapons of the spirit, should you prefer. The churches have been altogether too timid, not only in joining this movement, but in bringing their gifts of discernment and spirit. Consider the tactics of liturgy, prayer, fasting, song, even ancient rites of exorcism.

Cheryl Kirk-Duggan has marshalled a substantial Womanist analysis of the Black Spirituals, and called it *Exorcising Evil.*[8] Her own pilgrimage in the terrain she counted "a sacramental worship experience." The Spirituals, those songs created by African American slaves and eventually reworked by freedom struggle activists (with echoes and built-upon refrains) are essentially a body of liturgical action that disempowers the demonic of slavery and white male supremacy, and opens human space for Black lives.

Add that, the current movement can be seen to draw on other traditions, African, Indigenous, and hip hop spirituality, among them, to build

---

7. See Wink, *Naming the Powers*; Wink, *Unmasking the Powers* is virtually devoted to this question.

8. Kirk-Duggan, *Exorcising Evil.*

community and engage this power. Music and rhythm, poetry and art builds, invocation of the ancestors, ceremony and procession are among the strategies for confronting its possessive spiritual claims.

The assault on Black bodies and Black lives is obvious. Less clear, perhaps, is the dehumanization it wrecks upon white folks. We (I write from such a personal and social location) are deadened, emotionally incapacitated, in perpetual denial, dreading of shame, in bondage to the seductions of ersatz privilege. Dispossession entails confession of complicity in our own bondage. We live in a system of white supremacy, and white supremacy lives in us.

Recent work on race trauma indicates that white supremacy inflicts and encodes itself in our bodies. Differently so in Black, white, and police bodies, bypassing our reason and rationality.[9] This is a spiritual imprint. Confronting the systemic principality of white racism begins with and is inseparable from our own healing and transformation.

As I move to conclude this essay, the United States Senate has failed to convict Donald John Trump of inciting the white supremacist mob that invaded and assaulted the Capitol. I have been rereading what I wrote in the days after his inauguration, an analysis of the principalities at work in his election and transition to power. In utter modesty, that form of theological analysis enabled me verily to prescience.[10] In relation to the present discussion, I cite the following:

> Who would have imagined that the most immediate and caustic outcome of the 2016 presidential campaign, actually culminated and triggered by the election itself, would be the unleashing of a spirit of domination? Institutionally and street level. The worst impulses of human beings, however suppressed, were conjured, summoned, and granted a free rein. Fear, hatred, contempt, all were sent on newly appointed errands, house to house. White supremacy is public like guns in an open carry state. Misogyny is a legitimate political position. . . . Hate crimes spike. . . . The Attorney General says [local police forces] will no longer be monitored by the Federal Government in the effort to reduce killings at the hands of law enforcement. Such constraints only reduce

---

9. See Menakem, *My Grandmother's Hands*.

10. See "Trump Powers: Principalities and the Presidency," in Wylie-Kellermann, *Principalities in Particular*, 259–88, especially sections "Trump as a Principality," "A Spirit Unleashed," "Trump Theology: the Devotion of National Populism," "Babel, Troll Storms and the Principality of Social Media," and "Truth Warriors and the Renewal of Vocation."

effectiveness, he says. . . . Black and brown bodies will feel the heat.[11]

As a power white supremacy is foundational, even in the Constitution and the slave-built Capitol, but in summoning it publicly, Mr. Trump has been its pitiful victim, utterly dehumanized. He conjured and nourished, bid and unleashed white supremacy in a true collusion with his campaign and administration, never mind his delusional attempt to retain power. He armed, signaled, and marshalled it. But in fact, it used him in its latest rise. Wrapped him around its finger. Worked its dehumanizing way.

Ironically, it contributed to his downfall. The denial of death and the systematic suppression of mourning, are aspects of white imperial culture and religion. You can't claim the "benefits" of Indigenous genocide and Black slavery without being in constant denial about the death present beneath everything. Grief is suppressed lest it overwhelm white folks as shame.

From the beginning of the COVID crisis, Donald Trump's incapacity for empathy was all but notorious. He seemed spiritually unable to grieve, let alone lead a nation in mourning. This was more than a political strategy that focuses on the health of the economy (a power in itself) over human beings. It's a sincere lack of emotional intelligence, part of the incompleteness of his humanity. Go ahead and contrast him with Abraham Lincoln pastoring a nation in the Gettysburg Address, or Barack Obama tearfully breaking into "Amazing Grace" at the Charleston, South Carolina funeral, but in this regard, Trump seems to be simply a stand-in, a representative, a cipher for the widespread wounds of spiritual/structural white supremacy. When COVID caught him, I was moved to pray for his life and health, his humanity, as follows:

> O Wind of Spirit who moved across the face of chaos,
> breathing life into creation and humanity.
> Heal this man, afflicted in his presidency,
> from the very illness he has unleashed in mockery.
> Defend him from the Power of Death by which he is so enthralled
>   and so embraced, as to set it upon countless others
>   whom we pray you protect as well.
> For the time and sake of mercy,
> withhold the wrath of your judgment and bring him instead
>   into the fullness of his humanity, painful though it be.

---

11. Wylie-Kellermann, *Principalities in Particular*, 266.

When his breath comes easy and he wakes, may truth dawn upon him
    like a bolt.

Let him comprehend, as if on the last day, in the fullness of light,
    all he has said and done,
    lies all counted, uncloud before his eyes.
Let him feel, even for the first time, the pain of others, their families
    their friends.
Grant him to know in his heart the falling club and the bite of gas,
    bullets in the back or the bed, the knee on a throat,
    the who of the carcass hung.
Cast out of him the dreading spirit of white supremacy, its guises and
    uses;
scatter from his soul the grip of its kindred demonocracies,
galloping war and impoverishment. Let their victims touch his eyes.

May he wake alive to the smell of autumn on the wind,
And in that scent remember all of Earth and her creatures.
And so suddenly, to weep for her dead, before the wild blown flood,
the thaw and its tide, the scorch and the dim of smoke.
Let him be at a loss for words. Listen and hear. Blessedly ache with grief.
And in silence, yearn for the
Day of Repentance and Reparation to swiftly come.
Know his wounds and their generations.
Heal him thus, body and soul.

All this in the name of Jesus
Who healed the blind,
    the rich, thought irredeemable
    and poor, thought untouchable,
Who for her mother's persistence, healed the child from the other side
    of the Siro-Phoenician border,
Who cast out
    the legion from the Gerasene in the tombs
    and the money changers from the Temple,
Who somehow managed to love enemies and urge it,
Who from the cross cried God forgive Pilate, Herod, and their minions
    for the brutality of ignorance,
Who taught us to pray: deliver us from evil.
As so we do, for ourselves and for others. AMEN.[12]

---

12. Wylie-Kellermann, "Prayer for Mr. Trump, the Human Being."

As you see, this is also a prayer for myself, and us all. Paul's admonition, even in spiritual warfare, is to nonviolence: our engagement is not with flesh and blood, but with the powers. In that sense, the enemy is not the racist, ourselves or others, but the racism itself.

Have I been clear? Electoral change is no defeat of the powers. They are embedded, deep institution, deep state even (as Trump intuited) in structures and spirits. It's like a multi-headed beast whose head is lopped off, but lives with heads to spare (Rev 13:3).

Is this the life-giving hope of the gospel? Yes. Without an unflinching look in the eye of the demonic, there is no other. And so we pray. And so we confess.

And is this gospel theology finding welcome in a new generation? I do begin to think so. Witness Grace Aheron, a queer Asian American femme, seminary dropout. She affirms what Stringfellow and Wink, white, male, theologians, have opened in this conversation.

> I find myself a curious magpie, willing to snatch treasures and wisdom as they fall from mouths and pages—to be taken back to the safety of my community, to hold them up to the light and see if their clarity is multi-faceted or just one-note pretty. . . . I imagine Wink and Stringfellow and their friends looking from Glory at their books in my brown hands, long neon-painted fingernails, topless and turvy on a queer beach in Queens . . . and they're laughing and shaking their heads in wonder at me, an unlikely heir. . . . If reading the Bible is a cross-cultural exercise, so then too, for the most part is reading theology. . . . The tools and stories of the past are only as useful as they are adaptable for the present times. I look into the face of the ones gone before and ask; *May I take these for myself?* Stringfellow, cupping my face, responds: *For goodness sake, yes, dear. Go.*[13]

---

13. Aheron, "Do I Want to Inherit?," 19.

4

Untethering and Retethering

Ellen Clark-King

THERE WAS A MOMENT in 2020 that I felt a futility and emptiness as I stood at the altar that I had never experienced before in my twenty-six years as a priest. It was to do with a whole range of things. Partly the experience of presiding at a holy table at which no one was to feast—we were livestreaming but not consuming communion. Partly the deadening weight of empty pews with no responsive energy to help lift up my heart. Partly the awareness of being part of an all-white leadership in a church that was too slow to attend to the institutional racism that corrupted its ability to live into God's calling. I felt in my blood a lament for God's people, and I scared myself with the depth of my own experience of alienation from my faith.

Which is not to say that I have never questioned and doubted. There has always been a healthy amount of agnosticism and ongoing reflection in my faith life—an awareness that there is much I do not know, much I have doubtless got wrong, and much that I have yet to learn (and probably from unexpected teachers). There have been long, grey afternoons of the soul even if I do not lay claim to the mystic depths of a true dark night. But this year was the first time I felt so untethered from all that grounded me in my experience of God.

And it was this untethering, this drift from groundedness, that gave me the perspective to see what it was that usually held me in place. It was an opportunity not just to reexamine the strengths of those tethers but also to look again at the God-place itself, the environment of faith to which I had been bound. I resonated with George Herbert's "The Collar" as I wondered whether this untying was a new freedom:

> I struck the board, and cried, "No more;
>   I will abroad!
> What? shall I ever sigh and pine?
> My lines and life are free, free as the road,
> Loose as the wind, as large as store.
>   Shall I be still in suit?
> Have I no harvest but a thorn
> To let me blood, and not restore
> What I have lost with cordial fruit?[1]

And yet I ended up in the same place that he did, even though the language he uses is problematic for my feminist soul:

> But as I raved and grew more fierce and wild
>   At every word,
> Methought I heard one calling, Child!
>   And I replied My Lord.[2]

So what I want to share with you in this brief essay is some of what directed my journey from the first stanza to the last. Some of what both gives me hope, allows me to continue in faith, and also some of what still shouts to me as needing to change if the church is to be a true home for God's people.

There are three things I am going to focus on as connections to faith and hope: incarnation, community, and the Jesus Prayer. There are two deeply interconnected things I am going to focus on with regard to the need for ongoing change: patriarchy and white supremacy. As each one of these could fill a book this will be an impressionistic sketch of a deeper reality that speaks from my personal experience and is the first word, indeed barely the first syllable, rather than anything approaching the last word.

So the incarnation. For me Christmas Eve is the holiest of nights, the incarnation the holiest of events, even more so than the night and event of the resurrection. For here is the divine action that made and makes me fall in love with God. I tend to think of myself as a radical feminist Christian but yet the core of my faith is still that God chose the ridiculous particularity of becoming incarnate as a Jewish male two thousand years ago. Which

---

1. Thomas, *Choice of George Herbert's Verse*, 66.
2. Thomas, *Choice of George Herbert's Verse*, 67.

is not to deny the presence of the divine within every human being, the fact that each one of us is stamped with the divine image and is called to live a life towards divinization. But it is to affirm that Godself was born into poverty and companionship, into family and violence, into the confusing wonderful messed-up reality that is this world and its human inhabitants. The embrace of vulnerability, of finitude, of suffering by the divine creator, womb of all being, inviolate and beyond pain—I need this to be able to open my heart to my God.

When I lament the chosen powerlessness of God—the refusal to be the *Deus Ex Machina* that puts an end to COVID and war and racism and poverty—the incarnation recalls me to trusting hope. The reminder of the infinite preciousness of human flesh, of the bone-deep as well as soul-deep connection of every human life to the divine life, of the divine echo within each human cry—this is the narrative that breaks through my lament and sense of futility. I stand with C. S. Lewis's Puddleglum on this one, as he commits to loyalty to Aslan and Narnia even when he is being made to doubt their very existence:

> I'm a chap who always liked to know the worst and then put the best face I can on it. So I won't deny any of what you said. But there's one more thing to be said, even so. Suppose we have only dreamed, or made up, all those things—trees and grass and sun and moon and stars and Aslan himself. Suppose we have. Then all I can say is that, in that case, the made-up things seem a good deal more important than the real ones. . . . That's why I'm going to stand by the play world. I'm on Aslan's side even if there isn't any Aslan to lead it. I'm going to live as like a Narnian as I can even if there isn't any Narnia.[3]

I'm on the incarnate Christ's side, even if there isn't any incarnate Christ to lead it. I'm going to live as like a friend of God as I can, even if there isn't any God.

And one of the reasons I am on Christ's side is the companionship that this commitment brings with it. I did not truly know, till COVID took it away, just how important the shared experience of worship, of communion in its wider sense, and of mutual in-person encouragement in the struggle for justice was to my sense of both faith and well-being. I am a strong intro-vert and know my need for times alone and in prayerful meditation; what

---

3. Lewis, *Silver Chair*, 156–57.

I hadn't realized was the depth of my need for companions on the walk of faith to give me energy, purpose, and direction.

The embodiment of the incarnation feels actual and present in a Christian worshiping community in a way that is different from a Christian praying alone. Theologically this has always been important to me—it is only together that we embody Christ in the world, it is only together that we grow in the demanding reality of divine love, it is only together that we can check our own self-knowledge and grow towards the true humility of seeing ourselves with God's eyes. But since COVID I have realized the experiential and emotional importance of it too. There is an energy in gathered bodies that is different from the energy of online gatherings. That's not a new or profound statement but it is one that is deeply significant for the Christian community's ability to live into its identity as the body of Christ for the world.

So much of the strength and energy of my faith relies on the faith of the person next to me in the pew or at the protest march. It gladdens my heart that the church is one of the few places where people can (soon again we pray!) gather across age, class, race, virtue, political, and educational divides to be one community of sinful saints. It is this that enables the church to be a force for positive God-wards change in the community, not the ministry of a few charismatic leaders. It is the imperfect support of broken and beautiful human beings for one another's faith journeys that moves us forward on our imperfect walk towards Christlikeness.

And one spiritual practice that has kept me in touch with the reality of this community throughout lockdown, and before it as well, is the Jesus Prayer: Lord Jesus Christ, Son of God, have mercy on me, a sinner. Usually in my prayer life I look for images of God that are not masculine and hierarchical—Christ Sophia is my go to mantra—but there is something in the Jesus Prayer that I find uniquely sustaining for my faith. Part of it is identifying myself as a sinner, something that helps me accept my limitations and step away from both perfectionism and inappropriate pride. I am not Julian of Norwich, with her unique, beautiful, and infinitely valuable insights into divinity; I am one of her "even Christians," a sinner among sinners, needing the forgiveness and grace that comes from other humans as well as the forgiveness and grace that comes from God.

The other reason for this prayer's central place in sustaining my weak faith is its ubiquity across the globe and across the generations. When I cannot step into a church crowded with people of faith I can still step into this stream of prayer and allow it to carry me as just one of an uncountable multitude of voices beseeching God for grace to change and grow. I can hear the echoes of other voices mingling with my own, voices of Christians who have faced wildly greater trials than any I am subject to and who have maintained their trust in God through it all. These are voices that tether me back to the ground of all being and allow me to lift the weight of believing from my own shoulders alone to share it with the Christian community.

And I know this Christian community is a sinful one, both in its individual members and in its corporate identity, and there are some ways in which I believe change is imperative for it to justly claim to be a place where Christ's nature dwells. The two areas I feel are most in need of urgent change are around patriarchy and white supremacy.

In her book *Invisible Women: Exposing Data Bias in a World Designed for Men*,[4] Caroline Criado Perez explores the ways that the world around us is designed with only male bodies in mind. From minor annoyances, like iPhones being designed for male hands and upper shelves being set too high for most women to reach, to life-threatening issues with crash test dummies being modeled on an average man and flak jackets failing to fit women police officers, the world around us is designed for men. That male is the norm is not some feminist theory, it's a fact of everyday life, and as true in religion as in data and design. Not necessarily amid the membership but definitely in the leadership and most definitely in the language and imagery we use of God.

Jesus lived as a man of first-century Palestine as well as being God incarnate. He was a man of his time as well as of eternity. The language Jesus used was the patriarchal language of his culture and religion—even though in his life and actions he broke down social barriers to welcome, teach, and learn from women. But Jesus also called on us to be open to the Spirit leading us into all truth. And one of those truths is the one known as feminism—the strikingly new recognition that women are of equal worth, value, and ability as men.

The only way I know to be faithful to the God I experience as Creator, Beloved, and Indwelling Spirit, and the only way I know to be true to Jesus Christ as the one who reveals God as valuing and loving all people with indiscriminate passion, is to speak of God in female as well as male language and imagery. I cannot be a priest and not share the God I know as fierce

---

4. Perez, *Invisible Women*.

mother as well as gentle father, as sister as well as brother, as indwelling all us women as much as all men.

The reason that this is an urgent issue for the church is one of social justice as well as theology. When we refuse to see the sacred in women's bodies, whether cis or trans, we fail to truly value women's bodies. When we deny the feminine in divinity we deny the divinity in the female—as theologian Mary Daly said decades ago "When God is male then male is God." The #Metoo movement shows us where that leads, as do the facts that women are still the poorest of the poor across the world and the statistics around abortion of female fetuses. Language matters. It's not a triviality it's at the core of how we humans see ourselves and one another. Misogyny will not be miraculously put right if we start using female as well as—not instead of—male language for God. But it will never be put right if we don't; if we fail to value the female as greatly as the male in religion as well as in all other walks of life.

The other area of change I feel called on to address is that of white supremacy and the endemic racism that marks the parts of the church I am most engaged with in the United Kingdom and the United States: the Church of England and the Episcopal Church. I speak to this as a beneficiary of white privilege who has never known what it is to face prejudice because of the color of my skin.

This is a complex and urgent calling. There is much to do: from dismantling narratives of colonization that support the Doctrine of Discovery, to positive discrimination in regards to church leadership that recognizes exactly how tilted the playing field is in favor of whiteness, to a fearless examination of the iconography and images of God contained in our houses of worship, to the willingness to voice repentance and pay reparations for the historic injustices perpetrated by the church. The church does not stand above the need for change seen throughout Western society but should, indeed, be among its leaders.

In his book *How to Be an Antiracist*[5] Ibram X. Kendi reminds us that we do not live in a "post racial" society but one that continues to be deeply marked by a racism that is contemporary as well as historic. He also identifies the fact that individuals and institutions can make daily choices to act in racist or antiracist ways: neutrality is not an option nor is any claim to be spiritually above this issue in some divine sphere in which race is invisible. God created us in our unique bodily diversity, and racial identity is, at least

---

5. Kendi, *How to Be an Antiracist.*

in the current iteration of society, a key part of that identity and the experiences embodiment bring with it.

The decolonization of theology and of the church is as crucial as the move away from misogyny if the church is to prove itself worthy of God's calling and of human commitment and devotion. I believe it is the particular calling of white Christians to campaign for such change, as it is our particular sin that has created the injustice we now see. The most basic of theological imperatives to love God and to love our neighbor are at work here. How can we love God with honesty of purpose when we put on God a mask of whiteness that obscures the true divine reality? We love an idol in that case and not God. And how can we love our neighbor when we allow oppressive systems to continue that privilege our lives, families, and experiences at the direct and deadly expense of others? An anti-racist church is the only church that can speak with integrity to its divine creator and to God's beloved human creation.

Despite the emptiness with which I started this essay I feel within a wellspring of hope. It streams out of the theology of incarnation, the mutuality of community, and the practice of a simple form of prayer. It flows into a commitment to making the church a sacred space that is uncoupled from patriarchy and racism. It is enough to tether me again to my faith commitment and to my trust in the God who I fall in love with again and again.

> But as I raved and grew more fierce and wild
>   At every word,
> Methought I heard one calling, Child!
>   And I replied My Lord.[6]

---

6. Thomas, *Choice of George Herbert's Verse*, 67.

5

Letter to a Young Activist

JIM FOREST

THINKING ABOUT BEING HOPEFUL in what seems a hopeless time, I recall myself early in 1966 when, age twenty-four, I was hard hit by a hurricane of troubles. A major factor was depression about my work. I was co-secretary of the Catholic Peace Fellowship. We were doing all we could to help hasten the end of the war in Vietnam. Despite the fact that opposition to the war was steadily growing, week by week the war was getting worse—troop numbers rising, more and more bombs falling, and ever more casualties, the great majority of which were civilian. "Napalm"—a bomb-delivered jelly-like substance that clung to bodies like glue while it burned—had become a new word in many people's vocabularies. Pictures were being shown on television of American soldiers using cigarette lighters to burn flimsy peasant homes. An Air Force general, Curtis LeMay, was urging the president "to bomb Vietnam back to the Stone Age." There was even talk of using nuclear weapons.

It was against this background that, on the fifteenth of February, I wrote an anguished letter to Thomas Merton, a Trappist monk who had become one of the most widely read and respected Christian authors of his generation and also an outspoken opponent of war. He was also on the advisory board of the Catholic Peace Fellowship. My letter began:

> *Valentine's Day has passed but no let up to the war in Vietnam. Love continues to find a different sort of expression there. . . .*

I confess to you that I am in a rather bleak mood. . . . For one thing, I am exhausted with ideological discussions. Earlier today I began to type out a few thoughts on your paper concerning protest. . . . But the question comes up, as I work on such a statement, Who is listening? Yes, you, for one—you will read my comments, and perhaps in some way they will alter your thoughts on some subject, or strengthen them. Perhaps it will even inspire you to write something. Yet even if you do, who is listening? Your words will be dutifully noted by some . . . those Christians who care about baptism and membership in the Body of Christ may be influenced by your meditations. But meanwhile murder goes on without interruption. This appalls me to such a degree that I get weary writing it down. Bomb after bomb after bomb slides away from the bomb bays. For every sentence in this letter, a dozen innocents will have died today in Vietnam. The end of the war is beyond imagination.

This morning I wrote a letter to the editor of [a popular Catholic magazine] in which I explained why a recent editorial . . . attacking the Catholic Peace Fellowship's condemnation of the Vietnam war was poorly reasoned and didn't come to terms with the reality of the situation in Vietnam. . . . I felt like a man in Germany in the 1930s trying to explain why Jews ought not to be sent to the concentration camps.

It all seems so utterly clear. You do not murder. You do not kill the innocent. You do not treat people like blemishes on the landscape, or communities as parcels of real estate, or nations as squares on a chessboard.

Yet no group seems more distant from these facts than Christian (and Catholic) Americans. I have all but given up talking to Catholic audiences about Christ; I simply talk about justice, raw basic justice. I think I've come to understand why natural law made its way into the Church. It was simply an attempt to ask us to be, if not holy, then just. At least that.

How is it that we have become so insensitive to human life, to the wonders of this world we live in, to the mystery within us and around us? And what can we do? What can be done? Who can we become that we are not? What can we undertake that we haven't?

I do not wish to sound despairing. I have by no means given up on this work of ours. But truly I feel like an ant climbing a cliff, and even worse, for in the distance there seems to be the roar of an avalanche. There is no exit, so I will not bother to look for one. I will continue to work, and there are the saving moments, the saving friendships, the artists, there is in fact the faith.

But I write this thinking perhaps you will have some thoughts which might help. But don't feel you have to have any. I don't wish to treat you as a spiritual irrigation system. But your insights have helped me gain perspective at past times.

Merton's reply was the most helpful letter I've ever received. As it was quite long, let me limit myself to the main parts:

Dear Jim,

Do not depend on the hope of results. When you are doing the sort of work you have taken on, essentially an apostolic work, you may have to face the fact that your work will be apparently worthless and even achieve no result at all, if not perhaps results opposite to what you expect. As you get used to this idea, you start more and more to concentrate not on the results but on the value, the rightness, the truth of the work itself. And there too a great deal has to be gone through, as gradually you struggle less and less for an idea and more and more for specific people. The range tends to narrow down, but it gets much more real. In the end, it is the reality of personal relationships that saves everything.

You are fed up with words, and I don't blame you. I am nauseated by them sometimes. I am also, to tell the truth, nauseated by ideals and with causes. This sounds like heresy, but I think you will understand what I mean. It is so easy to get engrossed with ideas and slogans and myths that in the end one is left holding the bag, empty, with no trace of meaning left in it. And then the temptation is to yell louder than ever in order to make the meaning be there again by magic. Going through this kind of reaction helps you to guard against this. Your system is complaining of too much verbalizing, and it is right.

The big results are not in your hands or mine, but they suddenly happen, and we can share in them; but there is no point in building our lives on this personal satisfaction, which may be denied us and which after all is not that important.

The next step in the process is for you to see that your own thinking about what you are doing is crucially important. You are probably striving to build yourself an identity in your work, out of your work and your witness. You are using it, so to speak, to protect yourself against nothingness, annihilation. That is not the right use of your work. All the good that you will do will come not from you but from the fact that you have allowed yourself, in the obedience of faith, to be used by God's love. Think of this more, and gradually you will be free from the need to prove yourself, and you can be more open to the power that will work through you without your knowing it.

The great thing after all is to live, not to pour out your life in the service of a myth: and we turn the best things into myths. If you can get free from the domination of causes and just serve Christ's truth, you will be able to do more and will be less crushed by the inevitable disappointments. Because I see nothing whatever in sight but much disappointment, frustration and confusion. . . .

The real hope, then, is not in something we think we can do but in God who is making something good out of it in some way we cannot see. If we can do His will, we will be helping in this process. But we will not necessarily know all about it beforehand . . .

Tom[1]

At the time, I shared Merton's letter with close friends. From time to time, when the sky was turning starless black, I reread it. In 1988 it caught the eye of Robert Ellsberg, then managing editor of *The Catholic Worker*, who skillfully trimmed it and gave it the headline "Letter to a Young Activist," the title the compact version has ever since retained. In the years following, "Letter to a Young Activist" has often been reprinted and translated, even been made into posters and bookmarks.

"Letter to a Young Activist" captures the heart of Merton's advice to anyone in a burned-out state or close to it.

The key sentence was *"Do not depend on the hope of results."* But what a challenge that is. Any action one embarks on is undertaken with the hope of positive, tangible results. One *must* have hope that what you do isn't a waste of time. But to the extent you *depend* on some degree of success, your capacity to persevere is undermined.

In his letter, Merton described peacemaking as "an apostolic work." Before receiving Merton's letter it had never occurred to me that peace work is of its nature an apostolic work—quite a dignity but also quite a responsibility. It was not an altogether comforting linkage. Few if any of Christ's apostles died of old age.

Merton challenged me "to concentrate not on the results but on the value, the rightness, the truth of the work itself." But it's not easy getting used to the idea that what you are doing is probably going to crash against a stone wall. The shift from focusing not on quickly measurable results but rather on the value, rightness, and truth of the work one is doing requires a major shift of perception.

1. Letter dated February 21, 1966; full text in Forest, *Root of War*.

One of the most helpful aspects of Merton's letter was his stress on keeping one's focus on specific people. "The range tends to narrow down, but it gets much more real. In the end, it is the reality of personal relationships that saves everything." I know that by heart and recite it often. It sums up what might be called incarnational theology. Words and slogans and theories are not nearly as important as how we see and relate to each other—the relationships we build—and not only with friends but with adversaries. In the context of peace work, it suggests getting to know, as best we can, the people and cultures being targeted by our weapons.

"You are fed up with words," Merton wrote. He was himself, he confessed, "nauseated by ideals and with causes." Ideas and slogans can so easily get the upper hand that you lose sight of the human dimension. Of course social movements require words and often use slogans to sum up goals. These have their place, but it's secondary. In a talk to his student novices, Merton—himself a master of words—once said, "He who follows words is destroyed." Like arrows, words point but they are not the target. One of Merton's main contributions to many people who were involved in peace efforts wasn't his words, albeit brilliant, but the witness given by his monastic life in which prayer and meditation were integral elements of every activity. Each day had a liturgical and sacramental foundation.

A major point in his letter was that "the big results are not in your hands or mine, but they suddenly happen . . . but there is no point in building our lives on this personal satisfaction, which may be denied us and which after all is not that important."

Personal satisfaction is certainly nice but isn't the goal. Martin Luther King, Jr. didn't live to see the realization of his dream. Merton didn't live to see the end of the war in Vietnam. But it's not important that we personally get to see the results of our efforts, however worthy our goals may be.

Merton was suggesting what I have come to think of as a cathedral builder's mentality. Notre Dame in Paris took nearly two centuries to complete—and now, due to a fire, is being rebuilt once again. But even in cases in which construction took less than a century, those who helped lay the foundations of a great cathedral knew they had slight chance of living to see their building roofed. Perhaps they imagined their grandchildren or great-grandchildren might have that satisfaction.

Merton pointed out that, like so many people, I was striving to build my identity in my work, defining myself by what I do. Far better, he said, to allow myself simply to be used by God's love and thus gradually be freed from the need to prove myself and in the process become more open to the power of God's grace.

Building an identity in one's work is so basic an element for all of us living in a career-driven, results-oriented, fear-wired society that it's hard to imagine another way of identifying ourselves. Asked who we are, we tend to respond with information about what we do. It's not easy to think in other terms, and indeed any more basic answer (what would that be?) might be embarrassing. But if what you do is rooted in attempting to follow Christ, in trying to live a life nourished by prayer, meditation, and the Eucharist, a life in which hospitality and love of neighbor are major elements, that rock-hard foundation may not only keep you going in dark times but actually make your work more effective.

The great thing, Merton pointed out, "is to live, not to pour out your life in the service of a myth: and we turn the best things into myths." Merton meant myth in the sense of a purely fictitious narrative. In my own case the problem was not so much making myself the servant of a myth (truth often comes wrapped in myth), but the servant of an ideology. Even Christianity can be flattened into an ideology—a loveless closed system of ideas, theories, and concepts, every spark of divine fire smothered in footnotes.

In place of being dominated by causes, Merton advised, all that was needed was just to serve Christ's truth. It is finally Christ's truth that matters. Trying to live within Christ's truth certainly doesn't mean we will live a life without failure. There is a reason that Christianity's main symbol is the cross. But it may help prevent frustration and disappointment from becoming despair.

The ultimate hope, Merton concluded, isn't in something we think we can do but in God who is weaving gold out of the straw of our imperfect efforts, but doing this in ways we cannot see at the time.

6

In Search of Kindness

Emma Percy

OVER RECENT YEARS I have been thinking about resilience. In my work with students as a college chaplain, the term has become a buzzword; how do we encourage resilience? In my personal life over this time I have faced the illness and death of a much-loved younger brother, and a protracted experience of seeing a loved one systematically bullied and psychologically harmed. On top of all of this, like everyone else, I have faced all the restrictions and fears of this global pandemic. There have been plenty of things to fear: illness, death, loss of reputation, money, home, and friends. People comment on my resilience; the capacity to live through these situations with what I call "fortitude." My response is that I have been sustained by the kindness of others.

Fortitude is the virtue that enables us to live through fearful times. It is the balance between a recklessness that is fearless, and a despair that makes us unable to cope. One of the key things that helps to practice fortitude and build resilience is kindness. In the face of fear, we long for kindness. We are sustained by those who treat us kindly. Sharon Welch, writing about resistance to injustice, stresses the importance of communities of love and mutual respect. What Martin Luther King, Jr. referred to as "the beloved community"—the space of justice and joy. Welch states, "The ability to resist—the continual reminders that it is possible and worthwhile—is sustained by the creation of alternative structures, by a community in which the love that compels and sustains resistance is fully expressed."[1]

Yet sadly, in the face of fear, many become *un*-kind. There is the deliberate cruelty of those who seek to hurt; and then the cruelty of turning away, refusing to look or to do anything to mitigate what is going on. Self-protection means, for many, that walking by on the other side of the road seems not just desirable but advisable. Finding the courage to be kind is about recognizing the worth of the other. Kindness doesn't need to be manifested in grand gestures. The smallest acts can help to bring comfort to literally strengthen those who are struggling. I have learnt to welcome and savour each act of kindness.

The term kindness comes from the word for *kin*. Kin-dness (if you like) is about showing a kindred spirit, recognizing the other as a fellow human being. It needs some careful thought. Over the years I have struggled with those offering shows of piety and prayer—but that is very different from kindness. By this I mean those who have assured me of prayers whilst keeping me firmly at a distance, or told me I am "in their thoughts," whilst failing to reach out in any tangible way. Such messages can feel hurtfully patronizing rather than empathizing. I am glad people pray, but that message needs to come with some genuine sense of understanding, some recognition of who I am and the fears I am living through.

The kind woman who packs together an envelope of different chocolate bars with an interesting postcard each month, leaving it in my college pigeonhole, feeds my heart as well as my stomach with tastes of joy. Kindness requires curiosity and some imagination. What is it like for the one who is suffering? Maybe I can do little to change what they are going through, but I could offer a little moment of sweetness, a gesture of connectivity, something humane?

We have seen a new interest in kindness during the months of the COVID-19 pandemic. Simple acts of fetching shopping for neighbors, making gift parcels for tired frontline medical staff, checking in on the lonely and shielding, have all been recognized as good things to do. Kindness has been seen as something positive. We have heard the language of our common humanity, and been urged to accept all of the restrictions for the sake of others. Small acts of kindness and grand gestures of sacrificial service have been foregrounded in a way that we are not used to, and they have given us hope. Will it be possible for this to continue in the world beyond the

1. Welch, *Feminist Ethic of Risk*, 80.

pandemic? Or will selfishness once again become the dominant model of our humanity?

In their book *On Kindness*, Phillips and Taylor note that by the end of the nineteenth century kindness had become a feminine trait: "To yield to kindness was feebly feminine. This derogatory association of women with kindness persisted into the modern age."[2]

This association of kindness with women, and as a soft, almost weak, way of living, has been dominant in our modern age. We are taught to prize independence and to see our need of others' kindness as a form of inadequacy. The equality movement has too often meant that to succeed in modern life, women needed to become more like men, such that kindness became a less-valued attribute for success.

What if that could be altered? What happens when people receive kindness to help them face fear? Perhaps we need to look for help in this from those who have found resilience through kindness and then show kindness to others. If we practice it, may we also learn to pass it on?

As a practical theologian, I find my theology gestating in strange places. During the long months of lockdown due to the COVID-19 pandemic, I was encouraged by my sons to watch *Queer Eye* on Netflix. I became hooked. This became my "feel good" place. When I felt overwhelmed with the uncertainties of the world on an international and personal level, I would stick on an episode and be moved by the sheer warmth and kindness that flooded into our living room. For those who have no idea what I am talking about, *Queer Eye* is basically a makeover program. Individuals whose lives have got stuck for some reason (often rooted in trauma, tragedy or pain) are nominated to welcome the Fab Five into their life for a week. The five are men with expertise in grooming, clothes, design, food, and wellbeing. They are all gay. This gives them a freedom to be different. The result is transformational and life-changing.

In each episode we meet an individual who is stuck. The reasons for this are different, but usually result in a difficulty in focusing on self-care. Sometimes they are so fixated on helping others they do not know how to look after themselves. Sometimes they are stuck in a time warp, unable to let go of the past and live confidently in the present. Often there is fear, either in the past or the future. Fear of rejection, fear of not being good enough, fear that if they stop for a minute everything will fall apart, fear of loss and grief. Some of these fears arise out of genuine experiences of

---

2. Phillips and Taylor, *On Kindness*, 42.

rejection or failure or loss. Others are projections shaped by inadequate self-esteem or patterns of upbringing that suggested any focus on the self was selfish. Many of them find it hard to ask for help. We see how often fear can paralyze people or leave them trying to hang on to an idea of themselves which is long out of date. We see how fear can cause them to reject help from the people who love and care for them, believing that any kind of dependency is weakness.

What moves me in this program is that these fears are always met with compassion and kindness. There are no glib suggestions that life's injustices can be easily overcome. Yet recalibrating the relationships in your life and seeing yourself and others more clearly can unblock past hurts. Learning to know who you are and to find a sense of confidence is remarkably transformational. Having people tell you that you matter, that you look gorgeous, that you are strong, enables people to begin to blossom.

In pastoral theology the concept of wounded healers is used to describe those whose ability to empathize and heal others comes from their own experience of being hurt and then helped. The Fab Five are what we might call "wounded healers." These men have faced their own fears. Their queerness, and for two of them their skin color, has been lived out in a world that still has so many fears about people who are different. As they talk they share small moments of their own stories. We catch glimpses of painful rejection from families, of bullying at school, of tough times. We also get insights into the good relationships, the positive ways they have embraced who they are. We see ways in which harsh religious stances have caused deep wounds with one of the five finding it hard to even step inside a church building. Yet despite this he designs and completes a wonderful meeting space for the church.

These men clearly understand what it has meant in their own lives to be met with compassion and kindness, and they are able to express kindness and delight in those they meet. They show the value of relationships, of finding your family even if your own family doesn't want you. They tell people that they are worth it—not in any self-indulgent way—but in a genuine valuing of our shared humanity. They also spread joy. This is a generous program, where *com*-passion shines—warmly, like the rays of the sun. The Fab Five give; and they do so by trying to understand the person in front of them. They give to enhance and help. They give so that giving may be shared, and relationships built up. They rejoice so that people can learn to share joy. I know, of course, that it is television and it is carefully and skillfully edited. But that cannot take away from the sheer humanity and kindness on display.

As a feminist, I have spent much of my life trying to understand the fears of patriarchal institutions about women; in particular, the fear that allowing women to share in the leadership will result in the institution being "feminized." Often this is projected as some kind of weakness, a lessening of status for those associated with the institution. In the institution I know best, the Church of England, this involves a deep fear of women and of gay men. Women are welcomed in as long as they follow the rules set by the men. Gay men are still expected to suppress their sexuality in order to be allowed a share of the leadership. The shocking histories of sexual abuse and coverups have been exposed, leading to genuine shame and constant promises of culture change, yet it is not clear if the church knows how to make the change or even recognize how the fears about women and sexuality have been factors in the abuse.

In the church, as with many other institutions I have worked in, there is both a spoken desire for diversity and an unspoken fear of what that diversity will cost in terms of status, power, and change. I see much piety—constant positive comments about diversity—but often little genuine imagination about and commitment towards how to change. The wider society is calling for genuine change, not merely allowing inclusion only when it supports the status quo. The Black Lives Matter movement and the #Metoo movement have challenged Western societies to pay more than lip service to the issue of who counts and where power lies, and how much of the twentieth-century language of equality is yet to bear fruit.

How can we help institutions stuck in fear? Who can be the people to offer kind but firm advice? Where are the wounded healers that might be able to help the church and other institutions face these fears? Why do we encounter too many unhealed wound-ers in our institutions? Who amongst us can be the metaphorical Fab Five who can kindly speak truth to power, and also give gifts that can help us move forward with integrity in our uncertain future?

I believe we need to hear from those people who have known and experienced "othering," who carry the wounding of that experience. We need to genuinely hear the stories of those who despite the ways they have been marginalized have found the communities of loving support that enable them to give wisdom out of their learned experience.

For me, this means listening to those who despite the rejections, the sexism, racism, and homophobia they have experienced from the Institutional church, have found a secure place in God's love and an articulate faith of inclusion. These folk, and I include myself, stay in our damaged and at some times, damaging church, because we recognize that this is our family. We have found resilience through creating networks of kindness. We seek to bear witness to a God who loves all of her creation, a God who enjoys the rich diversity of humanity set in a rich diverse world. Finding strength in the kindness of God can help us to find a sense of kindred with those who are like us and those who are different. We recognize a common humanity made in God's image, a common family.

When you have been hurt, especially by those who should have been supportive, you need the healing that comes through the kindness of others. Ideally, family and church should be places of such support, but we know they are not always so. Many of us have created our own networks to sustain us so that we can speak confidently about the failures of the institutions we serve with a firm but fair kindness. We have, through no choice of our own, become wounded healers. Having faced the fears of rejection and marginalization there can be a new confidence in a richer vision of both God and humanity.

Some have written what we call "standpoint theologies," looking at Christianity and the world from different perspectives. We need to learn from these about the blind spots and narrow visions that are part of the church's past and present, so that we can acknowledge past shames and imagine possible futures. Some have written novels, created plays, films, and art to help us to find new ways of looking at ourselves and the world. These should not be special interest alternate theologies and stories but welcomed as the necessary correctives to heal fearful institutions.

As a woman growing up within the church it has taken so long to find genuine confidence in my full humanity before God. I have grown through feminist language in prayer and reflection, theology that speaks to my lived experience, the visible presence of women in places of power within the organization. These changes matter, but they have been so slow and so begrudging. How transformational it would be if a patriarchal church could truly acknowledge and repent of the ways women have been at best taken for granted and at worst oppressed and abused. How different if feminist and womanist theologies were read by us all!

The long history of othering women is connected to fears about sexual desire. This of course connects to the deep fears about homosexuality. The institutional church has taught men and women to be ashamed of their sexual desires unless they can be expressed in a heterosexual marriage. People have been rewarded for secretiveness, for a denial of self that is deeply damaging. Fear of exposure, fear of rejection and internalized shame is a deeply damaging wound that the church has inflicted on individuals and on its own body. Queer theology has insights to offer about embracing difference, challenging stereotypical views of masculinity and femininity, questioning our current idolizing of the nuclear family.

We have seen how gay and lesbian couples have things to teach all of us about what marriage means, and yet the Church of England has rejected that gift, suggesting that it should not be blessed. What would a church look like that was not afraid of human sexuality? How freeing it would be to be part of a church that celebrated all marriages. What can we learn about God and humanity from listening to the wisdom of those who despite all the efforts to shame them have found that in God's eyes they are good and gloriously made? The fearful church is terrified of acknowledging that differences in sexuality have always been part of human diversity. Clinging to the need to shame others there is a failure to see how shocking and unkind this looks to so many in and beyond the church.

The church seems to feel more comfortable in publicly expressing its failures in welcoming in people of different skin color. In the Church of England there has been a recent acknowledgement of the disgraceful treatment of the Windrush generation; the men and women from Caribbean commonwealth countries invited to come to work in the United Kingdom during the postwar years. They arrived in the "mother country," many as faithful Anglicans, only to find that they were not white enough to be welcome in the Church of England.

Yet it is possible to express sorrow for these failings without addressing the roots of the problem. It seems easier to look at a moment in the recent past than to address the long and complex history of colonialism and slavery. There are Christians across the world with stories to tell us that are shaped by their perspectives on colonialism and racism. The Black Lives Matter movement is another wakeup call to say, "Look at the world from where we stand." There is a rich and diverse theology; Latin American, Indian, African and black theologies written by those who have grown up with racism and the legacy of colonialism, all of which can and should challenge the white normativity of so much of our church thinking. We need to listen and learn.

It is a hard task to understand and repent of the colonial past that has shaped our society and still shapes so many ways our culture works. On a trip to India a few years ago I was shocked to see the white Christ-child with his white mother in the crib of an Indian church that traced its roots back to the Apostle Thomas. Yet this is just a simple example of the colonial legacy of a white church. For those, including myself, who as white Western Christians have grown up with a history and imagery of the church which privileges our story, there is a need for a reimagining of God, the church, and humanity. What would it mean for the church to really accept that Jesus wasn't white?

There is more. We need to encourage the theological perspectives of those differently able, those who do not fit the inherent class system of the church. Though diversity is preached there is immense fear of change. Above all there is a fear that diversity will mean an erosion of power for those who have held power as of right. This fear needs to be corrected by our gospel vision of mutuality and genuine interdependence. A broadening of the power base should be welcomed as enriching, not feared. Also, there needs to be a proper recognition that this change *should* be uncomfortable for many of us. There is genuine anger to be heard and carelessness to be acknowledged. Yet there is also hope. If we can start to allow the stories of others to change our understanding, we may find that in really listening to these voices we expand rather than contract.

The generosity of those who have been hurt by the established institutions is seen in their willingness to compassionately speak truths, to offer new perspectives, to unblock channels of fear. Philips and Taylor state in their book *On Kindness*:

> It is kind to be able to bear conflict, in oneself and others; it is kind
> to oneself and other, to forego magic and sentimentality for reality.
> It is kind to see individuals as they are, rather than how we might
> want them to be; it is kind to care for people just as we find them.[3]

We need this kind of kindness. Can we find the grace to really listen?

The Fab Five in *Queer Eye* regularly commend those they meet for their willingness to be open, to try the different clothes and new foods, to embrace new perspectives. I nominate the fearful church for a makeover.

---

3. Phillips and Taylor, *On Kindness*, 96.

You may nominate the institutions that shape your life. We need to let in the wounded healers. We need some compassionate critique from the standpoints of those whose voices have too often been deliberately excluded. We need the encouragement to step out of our comfort zone and learn from different experts.

In a modern world that is, albeit hesitantly, trying to talk differently about gender, sexuality, ethnicity, the colonial past and the diverse future, we need to find the courage to listen. Then we may be able to recount our faith in new and enriching ways. When it has truly learned to listen, the church may find that, despite all the signs to the contrary, it does have something useful to say. We may find that our vision of God is enlarged and our capacity to share God's reconciling love with the world becomes more authentic. We might become kinder and understand more deeply the joy of our faith.

7

Love During the Apocalypse

Daniel Joslyn-Siemiatkoski

THE PAST FIVE YEARS have been a kind of apocalypse for the United States of America. This has been a time of crisis and a time of revelation. Curtains have been torn apart and it has been more clearly revealed to us the extent to which American culture is in the grasp of the powers of sin and death.

The crisis we have been living through is compounded by the consecutive convulsions and traumas that have been visited upon us, like so many aftershocks of an earthquake. Insurrectionists storming the Capitol building; waves of mass shootings; police killings of black and brown people; antisemitic massacres; dehumanization of immigrants; imprisonment of children; pandemic exacerbated by systemic neglect of public health and the common good; a narcissistic president and craven political calculations. All of these things have played out in a cultural landscape in which there is no sense of a collective identity. Each event only deepens and exacerbates our divisions. Our disagreements now create not opponents but enemies. And enemies exist to be conquered, not engaged. The insurrection of January 6, given political and rhetorical cover by sitting members of Congress, made that plain.

For Christians this is truly an apocalypse unfolding among us because we are seeing the truths of who we are as a country. How can a Christian read the signs of the times and not perceive that America is a nation under God's judgment? And yet, the Scriptures teach us that an apocalypse is also an unveiling of God's own plan to act, to restore, to set right. And the question then is what are we called to as people of God, as followers of Jesus. What is being unveiled for us?

If the question before us is what does it mean to follow Jesus in times like these then the answer lies in what Jesus taught his disciples about how to view the world in which they found themselves. The world of first-century Israel was not unlike our own. It had its own share of injustice, enmity, oppression, violence, and disaster. In times not much different from our own, we read in Luke 10 that a lawyer asked Jesus in front of his disciples what must be done to inherit eternal life. Jesus prompts him to respond from the Torah with the commands to love God and love neighbor. And yet the lawyer presses the issue—who is my neighbor? And from there we get the parable of the Good Samaritan. A Jewish man lying helpless on the side of the road is ignored by those most expected to help him, his own kindred. It is the image of a Samaritan stopping to show a Jew mercy who demonstrates to the lawyer how to love his neighbor.

Samaritans were viewed as a kind of enemy to Jews in this time. Samaritans were the people of Israel who were left behind during the Babylonian exile. They intermarried with other peoples and developed their own distinctive way of worshiping God. When the Judean exiles returned, tensions and hostility between two traumatized peoples developed and deepened. Samaritans were viewed as collaborators with the Babylonians and deviants from the true worship of God. But the Samaritans also suffered under Babylonian domination and then the successive waves of conquest of the land of Israel. By the first century we have two traumatized communities, Jewish and Samaritan, at odds with each other.

With this background we can see more clearly what Jesus was trying to teach this lawyer and, by extension, his disciples. Can you love your neighbor when your neighbor is your enemy? In our own parlance, what if the man on the side of the road was wearing a Black Lives Matter shirt and the one who helped him was wearing a red Make America Great Again hat? What if our neighbor threatens our very life? In this apocalyptic time, this parable now takes on a fierce urgency. Are we capable of loving our enemies? Can we love our enemies when they are not just mere opponents but participators in our oppression? Can we love our enemy when they seem bent on a nihilistic destruction of the common good? Even if one might protest that the context of the New Testament is unlike our own, the challenge of loving even our fellow Christian neighbors now looms large in these polarized times. Even in Christ we are challenged by the question of who is our neighbor and whether we can love them.

The Letter to the Ephesians frames the reconciliation of opposing parties, Jew and gentile, as the sign of the transformative work that Jesus Christ performs. Gentiles who were once far off and strangers to Israel are brought into the life of Israel's covenantal redemption by the blood of Jesus. "For he is our peace; in his flesh he has made both groups into one and has broken down the dividing wall, that is, the hostility between us" (Eph 2:14). This is the "mystery of the gospel that must be proclaimed with boldness" (Eph 6:19). Gentiles, people from the nations like Babylon, Greece, and Rome, that had subjugated and oppressed Israel for so long are now also made children of God, like Israel, by the work of God in Christ (Ephs 1:5).

In the assemblies of the apostles in the middle of the first century, a new social reality was springing forth. Those who were once enemies were now reconciled by the life, death, and resurrection of Jesus Christ. But the powers of sin and death, still at loose in the world, stand opposed to this work. Hence the Letter to the Ephesians speaks of the need to put on the whole armor of God. In the city of Ephesus this was not an armor to wear in protest of the empire or to advance a specifically political agenda. The politics of Christ are not the politics of this world because they refuse to admit of division itself once people are gathered together in Christ. If we read the gospels closely, we will notice that when others try to insert Jesus into their own political agenda, he refuses. "My kingdom is not of this world," he says. "Give to the emperor what is the emperor's, give to God what is God's" is how he answers when questioned about the controversies of his time. Jesus argues with scribes and Pharisees not to discredit them but to expand the debate on who and what belongs to God.

And so, when Jesus is asked what it means to love one's neighbor, he offers the parable of the Good Samaritan. Who is my neighbor? Everyone. And so, the inverse question arises for us now: Who is my enemy? If we are to follow this teaching and to look towards God's own horizon, the answer is that those who come to me now as an enemy, become, by virtue of loving them, into not only a neighbor but a beloved.

This answer is the mystery of the gospel that Ephesians proclaims. Recall again the apostle's words: "For Jesus is our peace; in his flesh he has made both groups [Jew and gentile] into one and has broken down the dividing wall, that is, the hostility between us" (Eph 2:14). If Jesus is our peace, then there is the hope that this world can become a place where we only have neighbors, not enemies. It is this radical hope that requires the Christian need for the whole armor of God that this epistle invokes. It is this radical love that the cosmic powers of this present darkness stand against. It is this mystery of the gospel that the spiritual forces of evil in the heavenly places array themselves against. For this we need a belt of truth, a breastplate of righteousness, shoes of peace, a shield of faith, a helmet of salvation, and a sword of the spirit (Eph 6:10–17). We need this armor not to wage a physical war but to protect ourselves. We have no enemies and yet need armor. We have only peace and yet must resist assaults. We love and yet are at war. This is our truth because we walk as Jesus walked. We have listened and followed him. We walk the way of peace and find a cross placed on our shoulders. We are at Golgotha and yet are unbound in the Spirit. We are slain and yet live in Christ. This is what it is like to live as people who have stopped seeing their enemies as only enemies, even as the powers and principalities are against us. To live this way is to "make known with boldness the mystery of the gospel" (Eph 6:19).

Some might object that I am overspiritualizing our present context. We need only to witness the white supremacist and antisemitic groups and imagery of the January 6 insurrection. There are indeed flesh and blood enemies in this world. And yet, Christ commands his followers to love their enemies and to pray for their persecutors (Matt 5:44). And for what reason? Followers of Christ are commanded to this way of love because it is not the way of the oppressors, of the tax collectors and the gentiles. Rather, to love in this way is to "be perfect, therefore, as your heavenly Father is perfect" (Matt 5:48).

Our call to love is not a call to ignore evil and oppression but to name it and to work towards the conversion and repentance of those who would be our enemies. It is to recognize the fundamental image of God in our enemy and to witness to the truth that the grace and love of Jesus Christ can bind the powers of sin and death run rampant through our fellow citizens. Our love then in these apocalyptic times is indeed eschatological. Our love points to the future hope when Christ will renew all creation. Our love points to the persistent truth that those who share in the fellowship of Christ must ultimately transcend all earthly and political divisions. We are called to be renewed in the image of Christ and with that "there is no longer Greek and Jew, circumcised and uncircumcised, barbarian, Scythian, slave and free; but Christ is all in all.[1]

---

1. Col 3:11.

This love is not a passive attitude or feeling but assumes actions that make it real. And yet this is not any sort of reliance on human efforts alone, as if we on our own can simply will ourselves out of our predicament or merely persuade others to finally think like we do. If that were the case, humans would have already achieved a just society somewhere at some time. But there has never been a time or a place where the powers of sin and death have not wreaked havoc. For a Christian there is the conviction that the transformation we seek, the turning of enemies into citizens of the beloved community, rests in the power of God alone. It is God's work of grace, of empowerment by the Spirit, made known in the work of Christ, that will do this work. We are indeed agents of God in this world, but the action is paradoxical, counterintuitive, and not something we can on our own enact into being. It grows like a mustard seed and comes like a thief in the night. And yet, Saint Teresa of Avila reminds us that "Christ has no body but yours, no hands, no feet on earth but yours, yours are the eyes with which he looks with compassion on this world."

We are called into a radical way of being in the world. We can look to two icons of the struggle to see a transformation of the world in keeping with Christ's command to love, Martin Luther King, Jr. and William Stringfellow. In his *Letter from Birmingham City Jail*, King writes against Christian moderate leaders in Alabama who would have him leave aside his campaign of civil disobedience to win the freedom of oppressed Black Americans. Facing down the accusation of radicalism, King responds, "Jesus Christ was an extremist for love, truth, and goodness, and thereby rose above his environment." To stand in the way of love, which includes insisting that oppressors stop their harm, repent, and convert, is to follow in the radical way of the gospel that the world does not understand. The world does not understand it because the world only understands the vanquishing of opponents as unredeemable enemies. The way of love assumes in the end the oppressor can be transformed and stand with the oppressed. As King notes later in his letter, the sin of bigotry harms both the oppressor and oppressed—both need redemption from the powers and structures of sin and death in American society. And what is a redeemed racist, one who has been transformed by grace, but a scandal to this world? In the possibilities of such transformations the logic of partisanship and divisions begin to collapse.

But this redemption of the racist requires encountering powerful structures. This work is against powers that only God can really challenge.

William Stringfellow reminds us that racism, militarism, despotism, and all other forms of oppression are not simply a human construction but also a powerful manifestation in our material world of the spiritual forces of sin and death. As he writes in *An Ethic for Christians and Aliens in a Strange Land*, the paroxysms of racism, poverty, violence, and hatred that convulse the United States are not just a result of bad politics or unenlightened citizens. It is a sign of the power of sin from which the country must be exorcised. In the end it is God who alone can accomplish this. But Christians must live and act faithfully in witness to the power of Christ to destroy the powers and principalities stalking the land. Christians living by the command to love their neighbor, even their enemy, show forth the hope that God will have the ultimate say.

How then are Christians to live amid the seemingly overwhelming material power of racism, violence, and all other forms of degradation known in this world? Stringfellow powerfully cautions us to recognize that none of our political systems will fully solve this problem, although certainly policies that mitigate against harm are always preferable. The oppressive systems that close in around us are all different manifestations of death itself. And so, the Christian has no recourse but to claim the power of Christ alone against the powers of death. "To be [human] means to be freed from the worship of death by God's own affirmation of human life in Jesus Christ. . . . To be [human] means the freedom, in the first place, to love yourself in the way in which God Himself has shown that He loves every [person]."[2] In other words, to be human is to live the self-offering life of Jesus Christ in whose death and resurrection that power of death was destroyed.

Christians living out the radical, extremist practice of love stares death in the face and says "No" to its power. This way of life declares that Jesus is Lord and that death and all its demonic manifestations are false rulers. Christians loving during the apocalypse testify to the hope that lies beyond the powers of sin and death that have been unveiled. Christians daring to love their enemies, to see the possibility of their enemies' redemption and transformation by the power of Christ rebuke the power of division, despair, and destruction. Where the world perceives death, Christians see the empty tombs and those formerly in bondage to the strong man bursting their chains to rise in glory to a new life. This is the path that the gospel

---

2. Stringfellow, *My People Is the Enemy*, 148–49.

opens for those who would follow Jesus. This path carries a great price. This path is the path of our Lord.

8

Night Will Not Fall!

COVID-19: Opening to the Kingdom;
Challenge and Change in Uncertainty

Robin Gibbons

THERE IS A MOMENT in each of our own dealings with church when we are pulled up short; we ask the question, is this really what Christ founded? For a long time my own precarious place is what I describe as "the tightrope situation" of trying to balance a sense of gospel freedom with a loyalty to an Institution, which I love and yet also see as full of flaws. This creative tension has sometimes led to a less than prophetic stance of compromise, which I try to excuse by reflecting on the parable of the wheat and tares (Matt 13). But that's not good enough, for as Christian and priest, I am called to sow seed and harvest all, good and bad, then with knowledge and experience supposedly able to separate out the wheat from the weeds and winnow the chaff. It has often been difficult to see what is wheat or weeds in the pastoral situation as Christ's sower or harvester. I question myself as a presbyter, am I a failure? The answer is actually no! There is nothing new in this dilemma, for every age produces saints who grow a fertile, fruitful crop of holiness and vision in the soil of earthly life, and sinners who cause confusion or simply conflate and corrupt the gospel into their own interpretation of a self-indulgent life with unpleasant consequences for others, but it is the Lord's harvest—not mine!

I am not pessimistic or confused at this time of trapped reflection in our homes often filled with fear of COVID-19, for it seems to me that there are still strong clear voices calling us to order, pointing out guidance and direction, not least loud echoes of the two New Testament Johns, "Baptist" and "Evangelist," whose voices still encapsulate what light might be found in a darkened world. They remind us that what we are called to do is prepare the way of One who is amongst us, hidden and not well-known, by proclaiming the call to love one another and help others discern the kingdom here and now (John 3:3–5).

Our world still has not learnt the lesson of the twentieth-century Holocaust and subsequent genocides, so the manifesto handed us by COVID-19, if we care to see it as such, is prophetic, part of the recurring call of Christ our Word to *metanoia*, to change, to turn away from a narrow view of faith and world, to recalibrate where we are on the map of Christian faith journey. People may immediately disagree with my contention that the institutional church has sometimes placed a narrow view of Christ into our situations and lives. I fear that is what many are seeing, hearing, and experiencing in the United Kingdom today. We have been given a challenge by a stern, unyielding virus, capable of immense variation and mutation. Do those of us who are Christian simply pray hard it will go away? Maybe we should, but we cannot deny its presence nor I suggest should we see it in simplistic terms as evil, punishment, or an apocalyptic calamity. It may certainly help destroy much life on our planet if we do not pay heed to its prophetic voice and change much of our lifestyle. Can we face the questions it asks of us? Do we even have the will and energy to tackle the way ahead? What is the role of the church of Christ in our uncertain future?

Christian Remembering in a Pandemic World

Christians are supposed to "remember" certain things, for at the heart of their gospel is the command of Christ, who on the night before he died took bread and wine and commanded his followers to constantly "do this in memory of me"! Implicit in so much of the New Testament teaching about Jesus is the strong indication that coming together, remembering, is an act that not only binds us together but commits us to a particular form of action, that of a different form of love. The foot washing by Jesus in John

13:1–20 is not simply a historical act, it is also a command to change, convert, love, forgive, and reconcile continually. That act is deeply resonant of the love of God that becomes mercy without end; but it is not without risk. It demands of us a hospitality of welcome to the stranger in our midst, to let our guard down and wait for a new encounter, and to understand risk as a positive step. As Christians we recognize these continual remembrances pulling us into the kingdom of God, linking us indefinably with the act they represent. So now a duty of remembering all that COVID-19 is, how it came into our world, what it has done, and what it means for life on earth, is essential for us in any future experience or theology of church.

In *Night Will Fall*, the black and white documentary about the liberation of concentration camps by Allied troops in January 1945, filmed by combat cameramen and produced by Sidney Bernstein and Alfred Hitchcock, the harrowing scenes of the Holocaust were considered too much for audiences, so it was abandoned and shelved for seventy years. Deemed too politically sensitive it was neglected and placed in the Imperial War Museum. It was not until 2014 that the film was put together and shown in its entirety on the occasion of the seventieth anniversary of the liberation of Auschwitz. It is harrowing, powerful, and stark, but it is important that it is seen, curated, and available to act as a defiant critique to any who would try to bury the past! The title is simply called *Night Will Fall*, a phrase taken from the 1945 voiceover at its ending which says starkly: "Unless the world learns the lessons these pictures teach, night will fall. But, by God's grace, we who live will learn."

That statement is also our question about our task to remember, as human beings, as Christians who have a mandate and commitment to proclaim the good news of the kingdom! Do we who live ever learn the lessons of history? The jury is out, I think, but this cannot excuse the church from examining its own role in what goes on. Whichever denomination we may be, our churches as institutions need desperately to address some pretty deep questions about our relationship with the inequalities and problems in society, not least identification with political and national groups especially when they are understood as repressive.

This pandemic is going to change so many things, not least the position of the poorer members of each country, economically and politically. Unless we as a church determine how we address these inequalities in wealth distribution, or look at the pressing issues over environment and climate change, leading the way by action as well as strong intellectual argument, the future very well might be bleak. The issues that faced a post-World War II Europe in 1945 are facing us again, but in different ways. Instead of concentration camps, we have dreadful situations across the globe where people are left at the mercy of powerful groups, other "camps" of deprivation, imprisonment, refugees, and poverty are there in sight. Harassment and persecution take different forms, often spread quickly and insidiously via social media to the great detriment of truth. It is this perversion of the "Word" that is Christ of truth and justice that we need to address!

Where now is that post-war hope and vision of a common intellectual, spiritual, and emotional currency for humanity as an entity of sisters and brothers? Where also the hope of Christians united together in mission? "Unless we remember" is a mantra our religious communities urgently need to play often at this point in time, because in so many disguises that fundamental right, the equality of all, has been chipped away. It is to our shame some church communities still play into bigotry and prejudice, which ought to have been eradicated long ago, but alas subsist amongst us.

We have to be careful when we discuss and talk about rights, not least in the context of church, because too often, especially in a media-driven age, people can too readily use the term as a tool for their own ends, even in courts of law. Within the context of religious groups this term can be, and is, used in prejudicial ways, such as defining LGBT difference in negative ways, rather than embracing diversity as something rich, life-enhancing, and valuable. Whatever happens in the evolution of this pandemic, the Christian Community ought to seize this opportunity for radical change in their understanding of personhood. With prioritization of resources, sickness, science, and care of the environment, it becomes even more important that our mantra of "remembrance" has at its heart the upholding of the foundation of human (and by extension, all) life found in the Declaration of Human Rights, namely that "All human beings are born free and equal in dignity and rights."[1]

We acknowledge the church of Christ has on occasion shown a lack of prophetic insight by not standing up enough for those who cannot speak for themselves! Despite this, I have hope because the church is part of a greater community, the kingdom. But to do anything much it will need to face some unpleasant truths in order to renew and reform itself! However, because of that deep, rich theological understanding of kingdom, it still has

---

1. United Nations General Assembly, *Universal Declaration of Human Rights.*

enough intellectual, moral, and spiritual currency to help change perceptions, attitudes, and hearts.

The Role of the Prophet

If anything, this time of COVID-19 in Britain has revealed divisions everywhere. The gap between rich and poor grows ever larger. The numbers of the homeless are up, what used to be termed "vagrancy" can be seen everywhere in our cities. Yet the burden of financial support does not come from the rich, but from that largely unsung, often ignored middle-income group, fiscally stretched, pensions under pressure, job security disappearing, now realizing that our future is going to be different. In this world the church of Christ's kingdom is still very much at work. That is important for it shows the beating heart of God is still present with us. It gives hope that amongst us are prophets who, impelled to respond to the Holy One, will find the strength to call us back to the gospel.

Pope Francis often voices statements annoying the rich and powerful, shaking up those who like religion comfortable and "safe"! Many of the poorer on our planet welcome and take heed of his ministry and leadership. He has consistently been a champion for the neglected, the poor, and the migrant. He has espoused the wider issues of sin in a societal and global aspect, trying hard to call out what he perceives is wrong, striving to get his own community away from focusing on a single issue or a world-revoking faith. Like his namesake he is a person of blessing. He asks of us to praise the Creator in all things, but also to repair the damage we have wrought in our little home called Earth. He finds favor with those who recognize the need for prophets, who follow the Spirit's prompting for the "aggiornamento" of Pope John XXIII, who have a vocation to "remember."

Pope Francis is disliked by those in his own church who want security, sound doctrine, who see the world as a place gone "bad" because it has "erred and strayed" from a supposed correct path. There was an image used in the pontificate of Benedict XVI, referring to an ecclesiology of church as a "remnant" that purified would be "leaven and light" in a tormented, turbulent, and fractured world. The metaphor of a "fortress church," to call it by another name, is found across the religious extremes of the left, but particularly of the right, where the "culture warrior" ideal of going into battle against the forces of evil gives faith rigor. This is a hard edge that does not sit well with Jesus's admonition not to judge!

COVID-19 is not our enemy. A true prophet, it has clearly challenged us at a point of balance tied to the critical issue of environment and climate change of which it is a warning to our planet. In this moment can we Christians also evolve, adapt to the world we live in, or is this the moment when we descend into extinction? If we respond are we willing to change all our tried and tested positions, restructure our lives, look again at the gospel, and involve everybody in servant leadership, not simply clergy and appointed individuals?

Ahead of us lies uncharted territory. It is a moment for prophets to regain courage, find their vocation, and rise up. It is a time to let light into our closed, fearful, upper room to experience the fire and wind of the Spirit; not to patch and mend the institution, but to rediscover the kingdom of God here, now amongst us. We are called to live the values of the Beatitudes; we need to do that in the kingdom now!

Night Has Not Fallen

Here are some things that can help us. A good, informed, open biblical trust in the oracles of the Holy One that allows all to feel accepted, no matter who we are, as a true member of the kingdom.

Then there is our real friendship with the abiding Christ, who has promised to be with us now and always, present to us in so many different ways, which we need to joyfully explore and integrate into our faith life. Let's look to our parent tradition of Judaism or our ancient Christian cultures where the hearth and home is a place for sacred things celebrated together. Christ is our light; he is also the warming "hearth" around which we gather. Let us ask for the Spirit's gifts of faith, hope, and love, reminding each other that we are "living temples" of that Spirit, holy people in a world that is holy. We are not countercultural, we are the branches of a rich, varied, integrative culture rooted in God.

Our experience of lockdown highlights an inability of the institutional church to celebrate in alternative ways. Yes, there have been online experiences, gatherings masked and sanitized, but are they a liturgy shared or a "performance done"? The committed attend, but others have been cut off. Unless we remember and learn, returning to an ancient domestic tradition of worship, less hierarchical, open and accessible, as well as giving available tools for building a "domestic" spiritual life, these others may never return!

I end with words from the homily of Pope Francis on the feast of Peter and Paul on June 29, 2020:

> Prophecy is born whenever we allow ourselves to be challenged by God, not when we are concerned to keep everything quiet and under control. Prophecy is not born from my thoughts, from my closed heart. It is born if we allow ourselves to be challenged by God. When the Gospel overturns certainties, prophecy arises. Only someone who is open to God's surprises can become a prophet.

So have hope, night has not fallen!

9

Simply to Live

SAM PORTARO

TOWARD THE END OF the second century the French bishop, Irenaeus, wrote "The glory of God is a living human being." If that's true—and I believe it is—then a living human being—each of us—is a sufficiency to God. All that we need do to fulfill God is live.

As a practicing and professional Christian, I have recited aloud, mulled in private, and written at length upon the words "I believe in God." Those words are not a statement of fact. They're a personal reminder. They're not meant to impress anyone, only to remind me of their truest, deepest meaning: I trust God.

Now in the seventh decade of my life, I confess that my only consistent spiritual practice is living each moment. If, as one adage puts it, the role of a Christian priest is to "comfort the afflicted and afflict the comfortable," I accomplish that simultaneously in maintaining the only truly spiritual practice is simply to live.

But living is seldom simple or easy. Neither is trust. Life is organic. Living and trusting are processes bound by time—engaged one day, one moment, one decision at a time. From the first tentative steps of infancy till the final faltering steps to death, we live and trust incrementally. Each increment demands choice—what to do, how to act, whom to be. And each choice presents risk, the ultimate risk being loss of life, end of living. Whether achieved through myriad small choices or one catastrophic choice, the result is the same.

The narrative of Christianity, the gospel culminating in the "good news" of Easter, has nothing to do with whether one believes in a resurrection of body or soul, or whether one believes in heavenly reward or hell's torturous punishments. The sole—and the soul—message of the Easter story is that we're free to live, invited to live, even commanded to live without fear.

The Jesus of the resurrection has precious little to say, yet wherever and whenever he speaks, he nearly always addresses fear. "Do not be afraid," he tells them. "Have no fear," he says. Why? Because those of his own day, and we in ours, are consumed by our fears.

Who me? Afraid? Yes, indeed! Fear filled my newborn lungs with air as I was separated from the only real security we humans know in this life. Ever since, fear has been a constant companion. Fear of abandonment, of losing my parents' love or my family's affection, drove me to achievements, some far exceeding my own desire. Fear of failure, and stupidity, taught me to shape letters into words and words into sentences, then taught me how to diagram them in complicated schematics painstakingly drawn with a ruler; taught me how to add and carry, and made a dog-eared copy of the multiplication tables so intimate a possession, when I was finally liberated from it, I felt its absence like the sick panic of a lost wallet. Fear of failure, and death by drowning, accompanied every swimming stroke from the first sputtering head dunk in the kiddie pool till I finally secured the lifesaving merit badge that nailed Eagle Scout. Fear of rejection chose my friends and that fear, in turn, shaped our vocabulary, our wardrobe, our interests. Fear roomed with me in college, stowed away in the VW, and sneaked into seminary. Fear sat in the closet's darkness with me and still flinches occasionally when the bright light of truth catches us unawares.

Who you? Afraid? Oh, my, yes! Because you're no different. And everyone knows it. That's why and how we do what we do to one another. That's how we get what we want, and how others get what they want out of us. Fearful of being out of step, we'll buy anything that promises salvation from whatever insecurity hounds and harrows us. Fearful of losing what we have, we'll give our precious vote to the candidate who promises to tax us least or give us most; listen to their ads.

It's not heaven I'm worried about. It's yesterday—will some old mistake stumble out of those shadows and ruin me?—it's today—will I say or do something to undermine my security?—and it's tomorrow—will I have enough, will I be enough? It's neither God nor the devil that's got me worried. It's you—will you still love me?—it's me—will I make it?—it's them—will they approve, or at least tolerate?

And Jesus tells me not to fear. Sometimes, maybe even most of the time, I do believe him. Why? I don't know—wouldn't be faith if I did. Maybe I believe him because every time I let go of the fear, I really feel I'm living—not just enduring, surviving, getting by—but living. Because the more fear I let go, the more life comes in. Because the more life comes in, the more I'm reminded that Jesus said he came that I, and you, might have abundant life, life in all its fullness. Not eventually, but now. Because as Jordan Kisner writes of that thinnest of thin places between fear and trust, "There's a membrane between imagining God's love as a thought experiment and experiencing it as absolute reality, and if you slip across it, the entire known universe shatters and reassembles itself to be more whole and beautiful than you thought was possible."[1]

My prayers these days are few. I'm less inclined to articulate aloud than to ponder in odd moments all innocent victims of violence throughout the world, especially the children. I don't recall when or where this petition entered my consciousness, but it likely emerged from life with my husband, who taught second grade for many years and often shared stories in those "and what was your day like?" moments that were part of our daily routine before retirement. As he recounted the tale of a child whose birthday had never been acknowledged or celebrated, or of one discharged to the school nurse for a change of clothes after an accidental incontinence, I could be transported in a flash across a half century and more to the locus of my own seven-year-old self and in that moment feel the abject rejection or mortification of the child.

This time-travel phenomenon is called empathy. It's a powerful emotional state, one that may be shared with other animals but it's certainly counted among the higher faculties of humankind. It's come to mind lately in reports of children armed and adrift on city streets, turning high-powered assault weapons on each other, murdering for game or gain; of children trained and armed for warfare in other lands, robbed of their own lives even as they take the lives of others; of mortars lobbed or bombs detonated in faraway places in the names of governments or gods. It comes to mind too often.

But it does come to mind and is taken to heart. And when that happens, we're practicing an ancient and venerable spiritual discipline.

1. Kisner, *Thin Places*.

Empathy—the ability to feel with and for another person—is a profound spiritual discipline, one to be commended in these fractious, fearful times. In the wake of tragic carnage, especially aimed at children, arguments flare. But those contentions are about adult fears and insecurities. Since I have no answers or antidotes to those, I'll remain with the children.

The birth of Jesus so inflamed the fears of Herod that the hysterical king ordered the slaughter of all male children under the age of two in the realm (Matt 2:16). Thus the first Christmas was bathed in the blood of innocents. While the biblical massacre and its contemporary counterparts each leave ravaged families in their wakes, the pain of parental loss is obviously insufficient to stem the violence, else the scene would not be so often replayed.

The active practice of empathy as spiritual discipline is the heart and soul of the Golden Rule that encourages us to do unto others as we would have them do unto us. It's a discipline because it doesn't come easily or naturally to us, and particularly so when we're enflamed with the anger that so easily transforms "the other" into "the enemy," replacing humanity and personhood with hatred and objectification.

It's when I return to the identity of my child-self and inhabit that being that I can begin to fathom—to discern—the awful violence visited upon the innocent, the child whose lack of experience (literally, "innocence") cannot begin to understand what is happening to him, what is being done to her—or why. It is then, in the active practice of empathy, that the enormity of sexual, psychological, and physical abuse is most fully realized. It is then that I am able to feel for and with that child and in that feeling, be transformed; I am broken. In that brokenness beyond my repair I recover my identity as a holy child, reach out to the loving God, and pray that if and when and until this madness be gone from the face of this earth, God be with every innocent in every place and hold them fast.

Deep in the heart of Chicago's lovely historic Graceland Cemetery there's a slab of North Carolina red granite incised with my name and my husband's separated by a simple stylized cross copied from our wedding bands between, space above and below to add the requisite dates. It's our gravestone, and a *memento mori*, which as our ancient forbears wisely knew, is sometimes a good thing to have.

Attention to death is neither morbid nor frightening. Fear of death, however, can hold us captive, take our life. Death and our natural reaction to it can be used to control; it's what gives the loaded gun its power and why the wielding of weapons is often less about greed or hatred than it is about power and control.

We fear death, ultimately, because it's beyond our control. Despite our best effort—and we do give our best efforts to this enterprise—our best science and medicine, arts and artifice have never succeeded in removing this threat, only occasionally postponing or temporarily denying the inevitable. Neither are we often or fully aware of the energy we invest in resisting this inevitability until we're freed from it. Rather like the denial of one's sexuality or bondage to an abusive relationship, the burden of self-delusion, social subterfuge, and public denial accumulates until truth reveals the burden's magnitude in its sudden dissipation.

So it is when we face death honestly. Christian contemplation of death isn't a goad to remorse, nor is it a wishful hope for a deferred fulfillment in some elusive life to come. Christian contemplation of death is the simple, honest recognition of human limitation, the acknowledgement that just as I had no say in how, when, where, or why I was called into being and brought into this world, so also is my leaving not in my hands. My life is, literally, out of control.

I can despair in this news or I can rejoice in it. I can let it cast a dark shadow over my life, or I can let it illuminate my living. In teaching us to pray only for daily bread, and to trust in God's provision, Jesus invites us to incarnate our faith in God in the honest awareness of the limits of our control. Surrendering the illusion of control and our futile denials of death's reality frees us to be present to this day and prevents us from tormenting ourselves about tomorrow.

To live without fear. That's the liberating promise of resurrection. The path of Lent leads to Easter, but Easter's not the end. The road winds on to Pentecost, and beyond. Then and now, to live in Christ is to follow the One who led the fearful from their hiding places, leads us still with the only commandment given after Easter—do not be afraid.

10

Trusting God in the Void

CHRISTINA REES

ONE OF MY FAVORITE film scenes of all time comes from *Indiana Jones and the Last Crusade*. Indy has discovered where he believes the Holy Grail has been hidden for nearly two thousand years and he is making his way through a perilous labyrinth of passageways hewn into the side of a mountain. Suddenly, he steps out of a booby-trapped passageway and barely stops himself from toppling headfirst into a terrifyingly deep and wide chasm. He will never reach the Grail unless he can find a way to cross the gaping void.

Mumbling out loud, he recites flashes of memories about what he has learned about the quest for the Grail, about needing to have faith. He pauses briefly and then, tentatively but decisively, begins to stretch out one foot above the dark abyss. In a heartstopping moment, he commits the full weight of his body to taking a step into the nothingness. Immediately, a narrow stone bridge becomes visible under his foot and with his eyes fixed firmly on the other side, he proceeds to walk resolutely across the chasm.

There have been times over the past year where it has felt as if we cannot see any way ahead into a better and safer future. It is as if a chasm has appeared in front of us where once was solid ground. Our normal routines and ways of living and working have been interrupted, challenged, some even destroyed. It's not just COVID-19: extremist regimes and groups, political systems creaking under the strain of trying to resolve complex and conflicting interests, and a climate wreaking payback on whole swaths of a race that has exploited and damaged it for too long—all of these things seem to have combined to create a perfect storm of anxiety and fear.

So much within us and around us needs healing and transforming. The events of the past few years, and especially the effects of the pandemic starting in 2020 and continuing into 2021, have forced us to reconsider many of our former ways of living, the patterns of our lives, and even to question what we think about ourselves and what we believe. If we have a faith, we wonder what we can do to equip ourselves for the "new normal," what will give us a renewed hope and a different perspective—the kind of attitude towards the future that the good wife in Proverbs has, who "laughs at the time to come."[1]

Although a lifelong Christian, about twelve or so years ago I had a revelation, a whole new insight into how I saw myself in relation to God, to other people and to the rest of creation. It is not too much to say that this revelation produced such a profound shift in my perception that it has given me a different way of looking, not only at my own life and faith, but at all of reality.

Ever since I was a child, I had always felt God's presence in my life, the silent, all-seeing onlooker, usually loving and encouraging, at times questioning or grieved by some of my behavior, but always *there*. I had experienced heartbreak and a time of questioning in my teens but came through that with new insights and a deeper faith. Then, in my early thirties, I went through a time of feeling somewhat lost, only before finding myself once again inexplicitly held in the "everlasting arms."[2]

As time went by, my faith in God grew and changed but remained resilient in the face of all the complexities of life. I always felt that God was with me, even through the inevitable trips and falls and times of great sadness or emotional conflict.

I cannot remember exactly what I had been thinking or doing that precipitated the momentous change of perspective, but one day I was suddenly given a picture of our true position in God. I saw all of the created universe, all that there is and ever could be, as being contained within a vast sphere—the Life and Being of God. Along with all of humanity, all other creatures, the earth, and all the infinity of space, I saw that I was within this vibrant sphere, this totality of God. Indeed, there was nowhere else where

1. Prov 31:25 (NRSV).
2. Deut 33:27 (RSV).

I or anyone—or anything—else *could* be: to be outside of God would be an impossibility. We all *had* to exist within God!

I was exhilarated by this epiphany of understanding. I did not have to go anywhere to find God, because my whole life and being was happening within the greater Life of God! I did not have to beseech God to come to me and be close to me because God was already as close as my own life and breath. I could never get lost to God because I lived within the very heart of the Divine. While my trials and tribulations were a very real part of my physical human existence, I now understood that I was experiencing them from within the Being of the One I had worshiped all my life, who I knew to be loving, just, merciful—the source of all joy, all wisdom, all peace. I began to appreciate in new ways the paradox that God is both infinite, transcendent, and mysterious while also able to be experienced as personal, immanent, and knowable.

Of course, I could not expect things to become easier for me, or to understand the fullness of what is to come, but I could now live with the confidence that all things that exist, at the same time also exist within the eternal life of God.

I saw that our attitudes of rebellion, our sinful acts, our suffering, all these cause us to feel alienated from God, but they do not alter the position of our spiritual reality. Indeed, our suffering can be seen also as God suffering with us, just as our rejoicing can be seen as God rejoicing with us, a dynamic Paul describes in 1 Corinthians, chapter 12 as existing within what he calls the body of Christ, all those who have been enlivened by the Holy Spirit and who follow Jesus.

In the book of Acts, when Paul addresses the people gathered in the Areopagus in Athens, explaining that the "unknown god," to whom one of their altars is dedicated, can be known as the one true living God, he quotes from the Stoic poet Aratus, who wrote that "in him we live and move and have our being."[3] For me, that sums up what my new understanding showed me: we have our entire existence within the Being of God. Though the poetry had originated from a pre-Christian source, Paul endorsed its spiritual truth, and commented that indeed God "is not far from us . . . for we too are his offspring."

The effect of this shift of perspective was that I felt a surge of fresh confidence. If my life is "hidden with Christ in God,"[4] as Paul writes elsewhere,

---

3. Acts 17:28 (NRSV).
4. Col 3:3 (NRSV).

then I never have to wonder again whether God is indeed with me, because I can know that I am with God! I can trust more and fear less, relax more and strive less, knowing, of course, that the same is true for everyone and everything else.

This change in perception did not mean that I became a pantheist, seeing everything as God, but I became a more conscious panentheist, that is, seeing God in everything, recognizing that I could see God in everything because everything that exists does so within the all-inclusive divine life of God, and, therefore, contains some spark, some spiritual DNA of the Creator. We may still be waiting for the fullness of Christ to be manifested and for the ultimate reconciliation of all things in Christ,[5] but we wait from within the Being who has brought all things into existence and who has given us life, knowing us and loving us with the same kind of love that exists within the threefold Godhead we call the Trinity.

Although the Trinity is never explicitly mentioned in the Bible, it is not difficult to see how an understanding of God existing in three Persons came to be developed. Throughout the Bible, from the first chapter of Genesis through the final words of Revelation, we see the Trinity in action; loving, creating, communicating, and working together within the very self of God.

In the prayer that John records of Jesus praying right before his crucifixion, we are given a hint at the dynamic within this interdependent relationship, with its neverending give and take of love. Jesus prays to the Father for his friends, and also for all those who will come in time to believe in him,

> that they may be one. As you, Father, are in me and I am in you, may they also be in us, so that the world may believe that you have sent me. The glory that you have given me I have given them, so that they may be one, as we are one. I in them and you in me, that they may become completely one, so that the world will know that you have sent me and have loved them even as you have loved me.[6]

I often feel that this passage would be better painted or danced or sung, rather than captured in words, so indescribable is the relationship Jesus is revealing in his prayer. I find it so amazing that Jesus wills for us the same kind of unity as he has with his Father, along with the same kind of love.

5. 2 Cor 5:17–19 (NRSV).
6. John 17:20–23 (NRSV).

For me, my shift in perspective, set alongside these words of Jesus, as well as so much else of what leaps out at me from the Bible, has given me a deeper faith and a greater confidence about the future, however uncertain it appears. I certainly don't think my insights mean we are in for smooth sailing, but I do think that we can go forward, buoyed by faith in a God who knows and loves us.

I also think that seeing ourselves as being in God also helps to remind us that all other people and the rest of the created world are also within God. That alone can transform how we treat our fellow humans, whether or not we share the same faith or political views or lifestyles. It should encourage us as we continue to work for the kind of world we believe is most just and fair, and it may help to keep us from falling into the trap of demonizing others or of dismissing them as beneath our contempt.

The downside of freewill is that people can and do make bad decisions, and that, along with the universal human vulnerability to "the sin that clings so closely"[7] means that we will still need robust systems of governance, justice, and law. But in holding others to account, we also have continually to hold ourselves to account. We are all prone to corruption, prejudice, and self-serving in one form or other. Knowing what God's will for us all is, and how much God loves us and must ache with us, can inspire us to keep going in the good that we do and in trusting in the goodness of God within us.

Knowing, also, that all of creation is likewise existing within the Being of God, can give us an even greater love and respect for the natural world and a more passionate desire to treat it as precious and holy. It seems to me that many peoples throughout human history have better understood our true relationship to God and the inherent sanctity of the earth. Western environmentalists and conservationists are catching up with what many ancient peoples knew: we and all creatures, our beloved planet, and all the so-called "heavenly" bodies we see in the night sky, share a sacred spiritual heritage.

We can go forward from the ravages of the pandemic, trusting that God hasn't somehow given up on us. We can work with other like-minded people to help to heal our world in so many different ways. Just as mass communications and the internet can be used for harm, they can also be harnessed for great good. We can partner with people all over the world to do what needs to be done, supporting one another and bringing what

7. Heb 12:1 (NRSV).

resources and expertise we have, to work with those who have greater local knowledge. I don't have to do it all, and neither do you—but together we can all support new ways of responding to human and environmental crises and of putting in place practices that will dampen the fires of prejudice and hatred, and lessen the likelihood of some of the natural disasters we have been seeing around the world—the ferocious wildfires, increasingly fierce storms, terrifying tsunamis and the melting of the polar icecaps. We can better hold to account corporations that produce waste products that damage our forests, soil, and oceans. We can support those who work within their own communities to encourage people who struggle to earn a living to choose alternatives to the endless destruction of the rainforests or the slaughter of endangered animals.

This may sound hopelessly utopian but so much is already happening and more of the good work can be rolled out by supporting those who are on the ground and who hold the vision of a fairer and healthier world. Perhaps as we emerge from the threat of the pandemic and all the restrictions so many have had to endure, we can look again at the vision of the prophet Isaiah, where he captures the truth of a world living in harmony—a peaceable kingdom.[8] We may never see a wolf literally living with a lamb or a leopard lying down with a baby goat, but we can trust that the picture Isaiah paints of abiding peace and justice, where everyone has enough and where there is no more war or strife, is true to our spiritual trajectory in Christ.

God's will is for a healed, liberated, just, and reconciled world. Keeping that vision alive and allowing it to soak into our hearts and souls can transform our own attitudes and expectations for the future. And, as we go forward, we can trust that nothing we encounter will ever be able "to separate us from the love of God in Christ Jesus our Lord."[9]

8. Isa 11:6–9 (NRSV).
9. Rom 8:39 (NRSV).

11

In Times Like These

Comfort and Courage for Change

Altagracia Perez-Bullard

"We've Come This Far by Faith"

WE HAVE GATHERED AGAIN, to tell the old, old story. We have gathered, greeted, embraced, prayed, listened, and praised. We have come together, people of African descent from many places in this hemisphere. Our accents vary, as do the details of our history and experience, but we are the children of the African diaspora; most, descendants of enslaved persons. And whatever the occasion, we are often heard to sing: "We've come this far by faith, leaning on the Lord. Trusting in His holy word, he's never failed us, yet."[1] Sung stridently, loudly, with confidence, often in the cadence of a march, we leave the gathering knowing that we have a goodly heritage that will sustain us, whatever may come.

This kind of faith, often seen among the marginalized, the poor, the oppressed, astonishes some and is admired by others. How can people who have suffered so, have such faith and hope? Is it simplicity or

---

1. Goodson, *Lift Every Voice and Sing II*, Hymn #208.

simple-mindedness? When Christians are among those who marvel, we give ourselves away as postmodern, privileged folks that have not availed ourselves of the depth of wealth that can be found in our religious tradition. The hope, courage, and even joy that can be witnessed among many Christians who have suffered at times an avalanche of difficulties and obstacles are one more example of the paradoxes of faith. It is the rich wine of those who have been pressed, crushed like grapes, who with few options, opportunities, or resources, have had to rely on God. They are beyond the illusion of control; they know they cannot manage without God. And God comes through, time and time again. They have a lifetime of experiences, generations of experience, as persons of faith, as families and communities that have survived, lived, and even thrived, because of the power and grace of God. They can and do tell the story of when they were attacked and afraid but not defeated because strength was given, resources made available, opportunities provided, and they saw through the eyes of faith God's powerful hand at work.

This then has been an occasion for praise and thanksgiving. It has also become the riches in their storehouse of experiences for when the next storm, the next trial, the next challenge presents itself. And in hard times, when they feel lost, they have faith practices and communities that encourage and sustain them through the worst of it. They share a faith and hope grounded in the lived experience of God acting in, through, and among them.

This lived faith has not meant, as some might think, a powerless, fatalistic attitude, where people chalk oppression and injustice up to the will of God. Instead, it has been the bedrock of justice movements, where sustained resistance and prophetic witness have fueled change in unjust laws and structures. To have this legacy of faith is to be propelled to action, moved to show forth in the world God's will of life abundant for all creation. Having been a witness to God's activity in our lives and in human history nurtures hope and confidence in the possibility of transformation. We live into the truth found in Romans:

> What then are we to say about these things? If God is for us, who is against us? . . . . No, in all these things we are more than conquerors through him who loved us. For I am convinced that . . . [nothing] will be able to separate us from the love of God in Christ Jesus our Lord.[2]

2. Rom 8:31 (Holman), 37–39 (NIV).

"A Mighty Fortress Is Our God"

The challenges of living and the ills of evil that plague us are not new. Anxiety about our ability to feed, clothe, and shelter ourselves and those we love is part and parcel of our human condition. Fears about health and violence, and especially in our day, the anger and frustration about the human systems that sustain and perpetuate problems instead of providing solutions, afflict us as they did our forebears. The ever-clearer recognition that the powers of empire are dedicated to sin in the classic forms of egotism, selfishness, and greed does nothing to quell our angst. Chaos reigns and it seems that all have lost their minds.

For some with the long view of history before them, the end of an age is visible. The denial of the sins we have committed against one another and creation itself will no longer provide even a jittery peace. Many have lived cocooned in a mythology disguised as history, that speaks of the great accomplishments of a primarily white nation without acknowledging that it was only possible through the theft, capture, genocide, and subjugation of peoples of darker hues. Again and again we turn to the tropes of the great democracy, the city on the hill, ignoring the bodies that paved the way to the top. Now all watch in fear as the truth erupts from a groundswell of protest. Voices cry for justice for all while others fear this is only the beginning of some great retribution for past sins. It is time for the age of white supremacy to end, for us to strive to honestly live into our most inspiring and aspirational visions of a democratic nation where all are equal. This change, this transformation, like all change, all transformation, is difficult and for many terrifying.

All the while this clear and visible struggle to live humanely with one another is nothing compared to the ways that creation expresses the truth that we are all interconnected in this great web of life. The environment, through poor stewardship, disrespected and abused, begins to be heard as climate change is eroding coastlines, producing increasingly devastating natural disasters and disrupting our means of food production. Our interconnected, shrunken globe provides transportation for ever-virulent strains of viruses, bacteria, and other microorganisms, magnifying infections into pandemics, and again our denial about our interdependence leaves us ineffective in responding to bring relief and spare lives.

The sheer magnitude of the problems and obstacles we face challenges our faith and our sense of hope. The truth, however, will not overwhelm; instead, it confirms what we have been told of old, our struggle is "against the rulers, against the authorities, against the cosmic powers of this present darkness, against the spiritual forces of evil in the heavenly places."[3]

"Leaning on the Everlasting Arms"

In the face of these real and present dangers, where do we turn for help? "My help comes from the Lord."[4] To turn to God for help, to know that the Lord will come to our aid, this faith-filled stance challenges us into a deeper relationship with the Divine. For far too many of us self-sufficiency is a point of pride. Never mind that it is a lie, we are all connected and not one of us can live without the help of another. This lesson was hard won through the COVID-19 pandemic, requiring the recategorization of low-wage workers into essential workers. We have been living, to paraphrase the early nineties hit by *Arrested Development*, "Tennessee," as if God were our spare tire instead of our steering wheel. As privileged people with many options, opportunities, and choices we are left in the face of these trials and tribulations leaning on our own understanding. Our faith was found wanting because we have presumed the driver's seat, and our illusions of control have left us anxious, as we navigate a road filled with potholes and boulders, all alone. Our fear is an invitation to turn and return to the Lord, to the one that says 365 times in the Bible, one for every day of the year, "fear not."

To hear these words and act in faith on them is to turn and renew our commitment to our relationship with God. We stop acting as if faith was another one of our possessions, something we have that we use when we need it. Something we are glad to have because our neighbors have it and we too can display it and be proud. Instead of having faith in our lives we need to commit to living lives of faith. Like the axle, we shift so that our whole lives revolve around our relationship with God, and from it our commitments, our goals, our activity is centered in that primary relationship. Hard times, fearful times, become the opportunity for us to remember what is important.

God will provide us with comfort and strength, that we might live into our call of making the reign of God the aspiration of our lives individually and as communities of faith. We can have a blessed assurance amid the storm, but we cannot pretend there is no storm while our neighbors drown. The gift comes from living in the truth about this broken world and the

3. Eph 6:12.
4. Ps 121:2.

power of God to heal it and reconcile it to God's self. The hope that will sustain us will not be based in illusion or denial, it will be based in the real, unconditional love of God for us, and through us for our world. We need courage to admit our dependence upon God. We also need it to face the truths that beckon us to act for justice in our neighborhoods and in our country.

Fearful times have the power to humble us, so we viscerally feel the truth of our dependence on God and our interdependence, one with another and with all of creation. Our relationship with God calls us to understand our relationship with one another as the sacrament by which we make outwardly visible our love for God. We no longer live oblivious of the lived reality of others. Our lives of faith give us the courage to look at all that is hard about being human, the work of creating a more humane world. The delicate, precious web of life that we are a part of is where we begin to tend, to care, to nurture, to be stewards. What goes on around us is our concern; we must care and reflect and respond in some way. We are invited into a renewed discernment of God's will for our lives on personal, communal, and social levels. For many of us it will be an invitation to take our religion out of the philosophical or cultural sphere of our lives and to be instead intentional practitioners of a faith tradition that is rich in power to respond in life-giving ways to death-dealing personal, social, political, and economic chaos. "Take delight in the Lord, and he will give you the desires of your heart."[5]

"Be Not Afraid, I Go before You Always"

What are the desires of our heart? Are we seeking the strength to carry on in the work of living fully? Or are we missing the comfort of shelters constructed to separate us from our neighbors, to hide the truth of their lives from view? Sometimes we say we want to go back to a simpler time, and for some that is the comforts of childhood. But we must ask ourselves, simpler for who? The temptation is to retreat into a deceptive fantasy formed by images of black and white television programming, of an innocence and simplicity that never really was. It is not God's will that we retreat from the struggles of communities for fairness and justice, that we turn a deaf ear to the cries of the poor or a blind eye to the lives of the unhoused.

5. Ps 37:4.

A strong identity as the people of God seeking to do God's will in the world is critically important. Listening and seeing with ears and eyes of faith, we recognize how God is at work in our world and we find our place, our role in that work of the Spirit. We offer ourselves to the ongoing, life-transforming work of reconciliation. This work for justice and peace matters. As we resist complacency and willful ignorance, we push back the systems that destroy God's creation: racism, sexism, classism, homophobia and transphobia, ableism, and every form of bigotry that nurtures fear and hatred in people. The depth of our relationships and our ministries matter because people are dying, are hungry, are struggling to put together the basics for their children because of the systems, the policies, and the politics that are maintaining the status quo.

Our faith will give us courage because this is heart-rending work that makes us vulnerable. To be open, to be honestly listening and learning from others, their stories, the contrary and challenging narratives, is not for the faint of heart. Yes, this is how we will learn and grow. We will learn about ourselves as we discover a world beyond our own comfortable surroundings. Like children who learn about their family's culture and practices when they go to a friend's home and discover that they do things differently, we will learn about our assumptions, our biases, our preferences, and our privilege as we engage others. What is it we believe and why, who does it benefit, who does it hurt, how does it align with God's will for life abundant for all?

We begin to see, acknowledge and connect with those all around us, maybe with a simple greeting. The grocery store clerk, the waste management workers, the receptionists all become visible, and as we see them, we wonder about their welfare: Do they earn a living wage? Have medical benefits? Get paid time off when ill? We care about our schools and libraries and hospitals. Some will raise the question in community gatherings. Some will work to increase voter participation. Some will challenge public servants in elected offices to prioritize equity. Others will walk the streets with those seeking an end to senseless violence. And in these interactions, in these new relationships, we will listen and learn about the reality in which we live, and about what God is calling us to do with our lives. Our lives become organized around a different matrix of values, so that it is not about our comfort and security. We are willing to be made uncomfortable, to live with discomfort and acknowledge the cost of discipleship, knowing all the while that it will encourage and strengthen us. "Then [Jesus] said to them all, 'If any want to become my followers, let them deny themselves and take up their cross daily and follow me. For those who want to save their life will lose it, and those who lose their life for my sake will save it.'"[6]

"Make Me an Instrument of Your Peace"

The collaborative nature of this work is a source of courage, strength, and hope. The challenges we face on a personal, communal, and social level can be overwhelming. There is comfort knowing that God is with us, that God will provide. Living into this knowledge with a community that shares this faith, knows this truth, and has this experience is powerfully lifegiving. Learning from one another, working together, reflecting and growing, praising God with thanksgiving, not only supports us on the journey, but it is a source of joy and celebration, even during difficult times. This means we practice what we preach.

We say we value community and yet our relationships remain superficial, even among the members of the body of Christ. Being willing to be vulnerable with one another so we can share our passions and our pain will deepen those connections we long for and need. Then when hard times come, we will have saints we can turn to for help. We can share our deep fears and concerns, we can pray and encourage one another when our niece is unwell, when our godson is in an accident, when waiting for test results. We are not meant to journey those hard roads alone, knit together in love of God and affection for one another; we are meant to bear one another's burdens.

We are also strengthened in our prayerful learning and reflection together. Taking the time to share our experiences, personal and in ministry in the world, deepens the roots of our faith. We share what we are learning from those on the front lines, from others we encounter on the journey, and from one another. Those of us accustomed to knowing, leading, and doing will be humbled by all we will learn from those who live daily in resistance to oppression, dehumanization, and despair. Reflecting and praying about what God is doing to us, through us, and all around us, will be encouraging in trying times.

Our spiritual practices strengthen our awareness of God's love for us and all creation so that it resonates through us in our darkest moments. We read the scriptures so that we can benefit from the wisdom collected

6. Luke 9:23–24.

there, but also so that we can hear the stories of people journeying with God through the centuries. We are encouraged, and we find ourselves in this ongoing narrative, this love story. We are nurtured in love, comforted in our fear, encouraged on this journey with a loving God; and our lives and our testimony share the story with those with whom we live, work, and play.

Our love and care for our children, our families, our friends, and our neighbors compels us to share these stories with them. We can share the Bible stories, we can share the witness of those we know, who are seeing the power of God at work all around them. We can tell the stories of our families. We can tell the stories that have made us who we are and that have taught us about our need to rely on God for strength and transformation. God's grace will be spread in this sharing, this truth-telling, healing, and reconciling, releasing us from fear, giving us courage, and building our confidence in God.

Christianity powerfully and publicly expresses its faith in the gathering of the believers to praise God in song, to hear the Word, and to live into God's will prayerfully, intentionally. The banquet table represented in our Holy Communion serves to feed our hunger and quench our thirst so we can live into God's call for us. The intimate and sacred connection with God and one another strengthens us to do what God "has given us to do." As we walk away inspired, singing the hymn or reflecting on the word, carrying each other's prayer requests, we go trusting in God and being the light of Christ. "Glory to God whose power, working in us, can do infinitely more than we can ask or imagine."[7]

---

7. Eph 3:20.

1 2

Faith in a Time of Plague

Martyn Percy

ON AUGUST 15, 1665, the weekly statistics on deaths in London were published. *Bills of Mortality* had been continuously published since 1603 by the Worshipful Company of Parish Clerks. By 1665 London had 130 parishes, and these *Bills of Mortality* provide a fascinating insight into how people viewed health, safety, and mortality. August 15, 1665, records that eight people died of "excessive winde," one person from "lethargie," one from being "frighted" (more were recorded in previous weeks), another from "meagrome," over one hundred from "teeth," just fifteen from "wormes," six from "thrush"—and over six and a half thousand from something called "plague." The register adds that same week there were one hundred and sixty-eight Christenings.

London's plague of 1665–66 recorded almost seventy thousand deaths, although the true figure is probably over a hundred thousand. Charles II and his court left London during this pandemic, and retreated to Oxford. In fact Charles II lived in the Deanery at Christ Church, as his father had done before in the English Civil War—a conflict that spread virally to the rest of Britain and Ireland, and claimed almost 15 percent of the population over a ten-year period. To say that the plague of London—the Great Plague, as it became known—was devastating, is to understate the matter. In just eighteen months, almost a quarter of Londoners died from bubonic plague.[1]

1. The information in these two paragraphs came from Graunt, *London's Dreadful Visitation*, and "Bill of Mortality from 1665 London."

We have tended to view this tragic pandemic of seventeenth-century London through rather rose-tinted spectacles. Our present political leaders have, to a large extent, paid little attention to similarities in the dynamics that made London a no-go area in 1665–66, and during COVID-19 today. Frank Snowden's *Epidemics and Society: From the Black Death to the Present* highlights how the massive increase in urbanization and intercontinental travel has exposed us globally to new pandemics. The warning signs were already here: HIV/AIDS, Avian Flu, Zika, SARS, Ebola—to name but a few. We assumed that the teleology of our highly-developed societies gave us immunities to relatively recent afflictions, such as polio, tuberculosis, and Spanish flu. In fact, some of these older diseases and pandemics—typhus, cholera, smallpox, consumption—have been surfacing again in the twenty-first century. Poverty, and cramped, poor, unhealthy social conditions act as breeding grounds for new viruses and bacteria. Malaria always thrives in environments where there is polluted, still water. It still kills five million children a year under the age of two.

The thrust of Snowden's book argues that pandemics have always re-ordered society. They invariably result in a "new normal" emerging. Out of the hysteria, superstition, tragedy, and loss, comes a realism that reboots society. This in turn prompts some fundamental political impetus for reordering society.

Our ancient forbears had a phrase we should remember: "*salus populi, suprema lex esto*" ("public health is the highest law, and all else follows from it"). So the marketization of health, welfare, and other forms of basic care runs enormous risks for both the developed world and the developing world. Healthcare, rather like education, is an inherently not-for-profit enterprise.

Why? Because everyone matters. And everyone eventually picks up the bill for the deprivation of education and healthcare in other places, because it will always directly or indirectly affect the whole of society. Politicians and people can try and evade their official and civic duties and responsibilities; but cannot avoid the consequences of such neglect. What we sow, we reap.

Snowden's book confirms what we know from other more popular studies of medieval England's health. Jack Hartnell, *Medieval Bodies: Life, Death and Art in the Middle Ages*; John Hatcher, *The Black Death*; and Ian Mortimer, *The Time Traveller's Guide to Elizabethan England* all give interesting insights into how the plague-pandemic of the time reordered society—politically, financially, and socially. For example, people born to serfdom might suddenly find they were beneficiaries and heirs. Pandemics redistributed power and money; they challenged authorities and prevailing social constructions of reality; they promoted new consciousness, and reordered priorities.

The common denominator across these studies is that there is not much one can do to escape pandemics and their social and economic consequences. Plagues come and go. We are seldom ready for them. When confronted by their reality, we often go into denial. The numbers that are published now on COVID-19 have as much impact as the *Bills of Mortality* in 1665. Inside, most people say to themselves, as they have done in previous centuries, "it won't happen to me." Maybe.

In the short prescient novel by Albert Camus, *The Plague* (1947), we encounter a story that narrates a plague sweeping the French Algerian city of Oran. Initially, just a few die; then some more; then even more. Panic grips the streets as the epidemic enfolds the population. No one was ready for this, and few thought any plague could draw near to them. The citizens of Oran live in a state of perpetual denial. Even when, like London in 1665–66, a quarter of the city is dying, they reason it will not be them. These folk are, after all, living in modern times. They have newspapers, cars, airplanes, and telephones. The people of Oran cannot, surely, perish like the poor wretches of seventeenth-century London or eighteenth-century Canton?

The hero of the book is Doctor Rieux, and his resilient humanism is profoundly moving. He does not buy into the religious interpretations of the plague offered by a local priest, or of the abrogation of reason by the citizenry. As the death toll peaks at five hundred per week, Doctor Rieux reflects on a child he has tended, but who has died. He reasons that suffering is unevenly and randomly distributed. For all the theodicy in the world, suffering simply makes no sense. It is absurd—and that is the kindest thing one can say of it.

How does Doctor Rieux respond to what is going on around him? He works tirelessly to lessen the suffering of those in his care. But he is no hero. As he later remarks, "[this] may seem a ridiculous idea, but the only way to fight the plague is with decency." Another character enquires of him as to what decency is. "[Just] doing my job," replies Doctor Rieux. In other words, duty and vocation come first. He is committed to caring for others in need. Little more need be said.

Should this, or any plague, panic us? Camus's novel suggests not, because panic is an immediate reflex response to a dangerous, but essentially short-term condition from which we can flee and perhaps find safety. But in life, there is no guaranteed security. From Camus, through Doctor Rieux, we learn the following lesson. That we need to love our fellow humans (whether we like them or not, and no matter how long they live for, or how much time they take to die), and work with courage and hope for the relief of suffering. Life is ultimately a hospice, not a hospital. We are here to provide some salve in the midst of desolation and despair.

As the novel closes, Doctor Rieux opines that "this chronicle could not be a story of definitive victory," because the plague never dies; it "waits patiently in bedrooms, cellars, trunks, handkerchiefs and old papers" for the day when it will arise again. One might think this is a depressing note to end this novel on. Yet I do not think so. It is profoundly humanitarian. In selecting this adjective 'humanitarian,' I choose the word with care.

Because to be humanitarian is to have a binding duty and concern for helping to improve the welfare of people, and this pulse can spring from moral and religious roots. To be a humanitarian can be religious and humanist (and neither party will mind which), because it is about valuing people as inherently precious. Or, as God would value them. The result is the same. It is the lesson of the Good Samaritan (Luke 10). Or the Ten Lepers (Luke 17). Goodness for goodness' sake: not for gratitude. Or for converts. Mercy matters.

Correspondingly, there is nothing explicitly "Christian" about Dame Cicely Saunders and her founding the modern hospice movement. Committed to the alleviation of suffering, she wrote to her patients: "You matter because you are you, and you matter to the end of your life . . . we will do all we can not only to help you die peacefully, but also to *live* until you die." Similarly, Chad Varah, a Curate from Lincoln, founded the Samaritans to help the suicidal and the depressed. All it took was the suicide of a young teenage girl, traumatized by her commencing menstruation, to restart Varah's vocation.

Both these examples are profoundly humanitarian, and the religious pulses within them are lively, if implicit. Sometimes it is only the shock and despair at the manner of people's deaths that leads us to review actual lives of others, and how to respond. Think Live Aid. Think Christian Aid. "We believe in life *before* death".

Like many people, I have been perplexed by the hijacking and hexing that has been going on in daily government briefings on COVID-19. Facts are true, and statistics are numbers you usually can't argue with. But presented in a disingenuous way, numbers and statistics can seriously mislead. There is one simple fact here: our figures for COVID-19-related casualties are stubbornly rooted in densely populated, poverty-challenged urban areas.

The real, underlying figures show that we are, as a nation, endemically unequal. Our epidemiologists find themselves unintentionally plagiarizing our social and political geographers mapping unemployment, disadvantage, and other indices of poverty. Pandemics have patterns (i.e., follow the money). What was it Einstein once said? "Not everything that counts can be counted; and not everything that can be counted, counts."

So I am deeply mistrustful of these rather specious government targets and numbers blurted out in daily dosage: "two meters apart, no less"; "100,000 tests a day"; "no, make that 250,000"; "more beds, Personal Protection Equipment (PPE) and ventilators are on their way"; "we are pumping another half-a-billion into our hospitals"; and "more nurses are coming soon." Throw in a weekly clap for the National Health Service too, just to give those numbers some ritual substance. One suspects that this "numbers theater" from Downing Street is there to distract us from more troubling numbers. But here we can only speculate.

Einstein was right. For what can measure the loss of trust by so many, when it only concerns the actions of a few? We need to be mindful of what we count; and always question the value attributed to any numbers we are invited to note (and those we are asked to ignore). Everyone matters. No one is expendable. There is no number or statistic in this pandemic that can be countenanced or justified. For all the talk of "spikes," "flattening curves," and "keeping the number below R1," there are going to be over fifty thousand preventable deaths. Which means at least five hundred thousand (perhaps a million) preventable bereavements.

One of the most heart-rending British Broadcasting Corporation interviews I have seen over the past months was with a woman in New York City who had lost her job. As have over thirty million other Americans. Like many who have found themselves unemployed, she lost her health insurance too. Most Americans have their health insurance tied to their employer. This woman was halfway through her cancer treatment and awaiting more chemotherapy. That is no longer possible, because she has no job, and personally cannot afford it. And even if she could buy healthcare, she would be bidding for slots that have already been block-booked and purchased by prioritized health insurers. She probably won't die of CO-VID-19, as she currently lives in perpetual self-isolation. As she remarked, testing for the virus is free in the United States. Treatment, however, is not. In time, she reflected, she is destined to become another number—but probably a statistic that won't be counted in this pandemic.

I recently took a funeral for a friend whose mother had died in a care home. Our funeral followed the protocols of the time. One son present, with his partner, the funeral director, and me. It was not the funeral he would have planned for his mother. Many more could have come, and would have come, were it not for restrictions on travel and the demands of social distancing. Yet we commended her to God's gracious care and keeping, and I thought of the words of comfort Jesus offers: "Where two or three are gathered, I am in the midst of them" (Matt 18). I thought of times when Jesus sat with the bereaved (Luke 8; John 11). I was reminded of these words from Thomas Lynch:

> I remember the priest I called to bury one of our town's indigents—
> a man without family or friends or finances. He, the grave-diggers,
> and I carried the casket to the grave. The priest incensed the body,
> blessed it with holy water, and read from the liturgy for twenty
> minutes, then sang *In Paradisum*—that gorgeous Latin for "May
> the Angels Lead you into Paradise"—as we lowered the poor man's
> body into the ground.
>
> When I asked [the priest] why he'd gone to such trouble, he
> said that these are the most important funerals—even if only God
> is watching—because it affirms the agreement between "all God's
> children that we will witness and remember and take care of each
> other."[2]

This vignette, as if we needed reminding, expresses something of Christ's own divine humanitarianism for those who were marginalized, isolated, and needy. The life and ministry of Jesus teaches us that to God, each and every one is precious. The *detail* of caring matters. As Luke 12:7 has it, "the very hairs of your head are all numbered . . . so do not be afraid, for you are worth more than many sparrows." Put another way, to God, no one is expendable. We all matter. We are asked to live as God sees this world: everyone matters.

---

2. Lynch, "Good Grief," 23; Lynch, *Undertaking*, 71.

Social distance between God and humanity is abolished in the incarnation. God is with us. "Do not be afraid" and "do not fear" are phrases Jesus repeats a great deal in the gospels. More than seventy times, in fact. We would be wise to remember that "perfect love casts out fear."[3] Yet also remember that the reverse is also true: "perfect fear drives out love." Our calling as Christ's followers is not to be fretful and fearful, but rather to become an extension of God's courageous, endlessly expended love for this world.

This does require quiet mettle, resolved courage, and compassionate humanitarianism. As a calling, it is inherently costly and sacrificial in orientation. Such love does not seek its own security, or indeed reward. Our calling is to express the continual love and risk revealed in the incarnation; to become like Jesus, who is the body language of God.

The philosopher John Macmurray wrote few books in his life, but one of his most absorbing meditations is on the essence of communion between individuals, groups, and societies. We are all connected. In his *Persons in Relation*, he also noted that it was important to distinguish between real religion and fake faith. The mantra of the fake variety, he argued, ran something like this: "fear not; trust in God; and God will see that *none* of the things you dread will *ever* happen to you." But, said Macmurray, real religion has a different starting point: "fear not—some of the things you are most frightened of may well happen to you; but they are nothing to be afraid of." "Do not be afraid," says Jesus; "do not fear." Have courage, faith, love, hope, and charity. It will be enough.

Harold Kushner's *When Bad Things Happen to Good People* (1978) sold millions of copies worldwide. But few recall that this best-selling book grew out of his own personal loss. Kushner was a Rabbi who dedicated the book to the memory of his young son, Aaron, who died in his early teens from an incurable genetic disease.

So the book was written by a good man who prayed very, very hard—but who still lost his son. Like Doctor Rieux and Albert Camus, Kushner knew that real religion is not measured by how we avoid suffering and loss, but rather, how we engage with it, and abide with and care for others who have lost even more:

> . . . people who pray for courage, for strength to bear the unbearable, for the grace to remember what they have, instead of what they have lost, very often find their prayers answered . . . [because]

---

3. 1 John 4:18.

God . . . doesn't send us the problems . . . but God does give us the strength to cope with them.[4]

We are plagued by all manner of numbers and statistics in our age. But even plague-related numbers and statistics may not be looking and counting in the right way anymore. We are asked to see as God sees. Count as God would count. One stray hair, one stray sparrow (Luke 12:7), one stray sheep (Luke 15:3–7): all matter. Everyone matters. No one doesn't. Each person is made in the image of God, and precious to God's sight and heart. What drove the humanitarian impulses of folk such as Doctor Rieux, or Cicely Saunders and Chad Varah—and many who currently work on the frontline of National Health Service and in challenging social care contexts, whose names will never be known—is what Einstein hinted at. Everyone counts, equally. No numbers or statistics that any government promotes on pandemics, and that suggest it might be otherwise, have any real place in this world. Nor in the world that is yet to come.

---

4. Kushner, *When Bad Things Happen*, 125–27.

13

They Joy in Thee that Fear Thee

Musings on Eschewing Dread

Lucinda Mosher

"What an incredible drug fear is." Anne Lamott, chronicler of life's messiness, once made this pronouncement.[1] From the first moment I read that, I was certain she was right. From my vantage point as a scholar-activist who specializes in helping individuals and institutions meet multifaith challenges, I see fear as a big boulder on the path toward healthy interreligious relationships. Fear can manifest itself as shyness. Fear may paralyze us—as individuals, as communities. Fear may obscure our vision and hearing, make it hard for us to perceive anything other than what we have already come to believe to be true. Fear may make us just plain nasty. And it is addictive. How folks love to overdose on fear! Some years ago, when my spiritual director caught me doing just that, she ordered me to give up "dread" for Lent. Forty days of opting for faith rather than fear: it was a sobering mandate. I recall taking it seriously at the time. As I revisit that directive today, what commands my attention (and what the Anglican tradition can help us appreciate) is fear's complexity. Here follow some musings.

---

1. Lamott, *Operating Instructions*, 109.

Note that my mentor urged me to eschew *dread*. That is significant. After only scant reflection on my part, I can say with confidence that when, in my teaching and advocacy, I mention "fear," I always mean "dread"—or its close cousin, "scared of." Yet, in actuality, for centuries, the term has carried other meanings as well. Consider its use by the great Renaissance metaphysical poet John Donne (1571/2–1631). When he was in his early fifties, having survived a grave illness from which he had come close to dying, he crafted an extended theological reflection with twenty-three sections, each containing a "meditation," an "expostulation," and a lengthy prayer. Given Donne's fondness for wordplay, it is reasonable to presume that this work's title, *Devotions upon Emergent Occasions*, has double meaning, with the term *emergent* carrying the sense both of "budding forth" and of "being a crisis."

In fact, *Devotions upon Emergent Occasions* is an extended reflection on the topic of fear. Throughout, Donne the consummate wordsmith plays with the term's multiple, paradoxical meanings. Consider, for example, a small portion of his sixth expostulation:

> O my God, can I do this, and fear thee; come to thee and speak to thee, in all places, at all hours, and fear thee? Dare I ask this question? There is more boldness in the question than in the coming; I may do it though I fear thee; I cannot do it except I fear thee. So well hast thou provided that we should always fear thee, as that thou has provided that we should fear no person but thee, nothing but thee . . . they joy in thee, O Lord, that fear thee, and fear thee only, who feel this joy in thee.[2]

Of these many iterations of "fear," which does Donne intend us to hear as "dread" or "fright" or "scared of"? When does he intend us to read "fear" as "in awe of"? Here is one possibility:

> O my God, can I do this, and dread thee; come to thee and speak to thee, in all places, at all hours, and be frightened of thee? Dare I ask this question? There is more boldness in the question than in the coming; I may do it though I am frightened of thee; I cannot do it except I am in awe of thee.

Whatever our exact translation of Donne, it does seem that he sees *fear* both as something to get beyond and that which enables something much to be desired. He says:

---

2. Donne, "Station No. 6," 34, 36.

> I lie here possessed with that fear which is thy fear . . . and there-
> fore fearful, because it is a fearful thing to fall into thy hands; and
> that this fear preserves me from all inordinate fear, arising out of
> the infirmity of nature, because thy hand being upon me, thou wilt
> never let me fall out of thy hand.[3]

Might his expostulation offer a means for dealing with our own situation here and now? In the twofold sense in which Donne uses the term,
"emergent" well describes the period 2020–21. Whatever their physical
location, people the world around found themselves in the midst of an
unrelentingly fluid public health crisis provoked by a fearsome virus—a
crisis which, in some contexts, was exacerbated by violence stemming from
systemic racism, economic disparity, or political tensions.

Episodes of mandatory shutdowns, isolations, and quarantines were
deeply upsetting, on the one hand; yet, on the other, provoked genuine
curiosity about individuals—adherents of one religion or another—who
choose deliberately to be solitary. As a direct result of such curiosity, I was a
featured guest on a talk-radio program for a segment on this very topic.[4] A
few days later, *America Magazine* published an essay by Gregory Hillis entitled "We are all monks now." Both the radio interview and the magazine
article underscored a point that bears remembering: the life of isolation
forced on an individual by pandemic or imprisonment is a very different
experience from a life of solitude as a monk, nun, or hermit. Isolation can
be imposed; solitude cannot. The hermit's vocation, says a friend of mine
who is one, is to hold two things in dynamic tension: the solitary lifestyle
with its Godward focus; and availability to any who desire spiritual counsel. So, no: pandemic restrictions did not transform us all into dedicated
practitioners of solitude. However, it did cause some folks—the talk show
host, Hillis and his readers, and my own students among them—to have
newfound interest in what can be learned from exemplars of the practice
of solitude about navigating fearful times. Time and again, imaginations
were captured by a profound vernacular theologian, the anchoress Julian of
Norwich (c. 1342–after 1416).

Julian is the first woman we know to have authored a book in English.
Entitled *Showings of Divine Love*, in fact, she wrote it twice. Her first effort
was a succinct account (known as the Short Text); she expanded it signifi-
cantly some years later (the Long Text). In *Showings*, Julian recounts sixteen

---

3. Donne, "Station No. 6," 37.
4. See McEnroe, "On Solitude and Hermits."

epiphanies resulting from six days of life-threatening illness spent in a bed positioned such that, as her fever raged, her gaze was directed toward a crucifix on her sickroom wall. The impact on her theological reflection was direct.

Julian's bout with grave illness was a scary experience in a life lived in a fearful time. Fourteenth-century England endured not only ongoing horrific diseases, but also episodes of catastrophic weather, ecclesiastical unrest, and warfare. "Julian never mentions directly the disasters of her age," one scholar notes, "but the message of her revelations is obviously aimed at providing some cure for the anxiety, confusion and guilt" generated by them.[5]

Chapter by chapter, Julian addresses topics such as sin, divine providence, joy, love, or the nature of prayer. Many will be familiar with her hazelnut parable, the lesson of which is that "God is the Creator and the protector and the lover." This small, nut-like object "lasts and always will, because God loves it; and thus everything has being through the love of God."[6] Here and elsewhere in *Showings*, Julian offers comfort for fearful times without saying so directly. However, in the concluding chapter of her Short Text, she takes up the topic of *fear* itself.

As John Donne demonstrated for us, the word *fear* can be employed in multiple senses; nearly three centuries earlier, Julian unpacked those various meanings. Fear, she said, can be shorthand for any of four emotions: dread of assault, dread of pain, doubt, and reverence. Fear-as-doubt is not useful, she explains; furthermore, God disdains it. Fear-as-dread *can* be helpful: dread of assault can be purgative; dread of pain (in the next world or this one) can motivate the sufferer "to seek comfort and mercy of God."[7]

Amy Laura Hall notes that "Julian received suffering as a kind of inoculation against dread. A reasonable response to the manifold traumas around her—recurring plagues, famine, a brutal aristocracy—would have been precisely to catch a contagion of terror."[8] What Julian models instead is the conviction that, in fearful times, the way forward is to stock up on reverence. This sort of fear, she asserts, "softens and strengthens and pleases and gives rest."[9] In Julian's view, "God is seen as always dynamically active

5. Nuth, *God's Lovers*, 100.

6. Julian, *Showings*, 183.

7. Julian, *Showings*, 169.

8. Hall, *Laughing at the Devil*, 13.

9. Julian, *Showings*, 170.

in the lives of believers."[10] Using analogy to convey her understanding of God's with-us-ness (immanence), she writes: "I saw that God is to us everything which is good and comforting for our help. He is our clothing, who wraps and enfolds us for love, embraces us and shelters us, surrounds us for his love, which is so tender that he may never desert us."[11]

In her theologizing, Julian teaches a form of the radical incarnationalism: the notion "that the incarnation had a purpose other than repairing the damage caused by sin."[12] Radical incarnationalism recalls that, through the story of the Good Samaritan, Jesus—Immanuel, God-With-Us—defines "neighbor" as one who makes a claim on us by virtue of his or her *nearness*. When we are commanded to love God and to love our neighbors *as* ourselves, we are (in effect) commanded to *be-with* our neighbors as Christ is with us. What I call the practice of *being-with* is characterized by Roman Catholic spiritual advisor Joan Chittister as cultivation of an "open soul." An open soul is beautiful; but when times become debilitatingly fear-filled, its cultivation is inhibited, as Chittister readily admits. An open soul is difficult to achieve in an environment in which the other is readily perceived as a threat.[13] The remedy is faith—which, a wise counselor has noted, is a process more so than a possession.[14]

Faith can be bolstered by accessing the strength of community. Returning to John Donne's *Devotions on Emergent Occasions*, we find his pronouncement (which I edit slightly): "No one is an island entire of itself; every person is a piece of the continent, a part of the main."[15] Consider it! Even in isolation, we have company. "Isn't it obvious?" asks the great Vietnamese Buddhist poet Thich Nhat Hanh. "Isn't it obvious that we 'inter-are'?"[16] It has always been so. It is up to us to make it visible. Sometimes, an emergent occasion is nothing if not the budding of new possibilities. Responding fruitfully will require courage—which, says Anne Lamott, is simply "fear that has said its prayers."[17] Courageousness, says poet David Whyte, "is to make conscious those things we already feel deeply and then

10. Nuth, *God's Lovers*, 109.

11. Julian, *Showings*, 183.

12. Nuth, *Wisdom's Daughter*.

13. Adapted from Chittister, "Xenophilia," 127–28.

14. Buechner, *Wishful Thinking*, 25.

15. Donne, "Devotion XVII," 272.

16. Hanh, "Please Call Me," 72.

17. Lamott, *Traveling Mercies*, 239.

to live through the unending vulnerabilities of those consequences."[18] Courage is living faith despite fear-as-dread. In turn, courage nurtures resilience.

Where persistence is firm or obstinate continuance in a course of action in spite of difficulty or opposition, resilience is more complex, more elegant. "Resilience," says acclaimed composer and three-time cancer survivor Abbie Betinis, "is a mindset born in the hardest days, when you're scared or sad or tired, when progress toward your goal is slow, and the barriers seem impenetrable . . . and yet you keep going, because somewhere deep down you know that what you're fighting for will be so much better."[19] Neither Julian nor Donne use the term: it had barely entered the English language by Donne's day. But both model it—especially in the ways they speak of fear-as-awe, of fear-as-reverence.

Indeed, I know that Julian of Norwich and John Donne often use *fear* to name a Godward attitude such as that of the psalmist declaring, "When I consider your heavens, the work of your fingers, the moon and the stars you have set in their courses, What are we that you should be mindful of us, mere mortals that you should seek us out?" (Ps 8:4–5, Order of Saint Helena translation). But much as I treasure their counsel, I can say with confidence that when, in my teaching and advocacy, I want to convey notions of "awe" or "reverence"—such as the mood expressed in hymns like "When I survey the wondrous Cross"—I will not call it "fear" as they might. When I mention "fear," I always mean "scared of"—or its close cousin, "dread." And, to eschew dread is to create space for cultivation of an open soul and embrace the practice of *being-with*. Eschewal of dread allows us to pray with reverent sincerity: "so draw our hearts to you, so guide our minds, so fill our imaginations, so control our wills, that we may be wholly yours, utterly dedicated unto you; and then use us, we pray you, as you will."[20]

---

18. Whyte, *Consolations, Nourishment and Underlying Meaning*, 39.

19. Quoted at Betinis, "Resilience," para. 1. For a compelling rendition of Abbie Betinis's street chant, "Resilience," performed by the University of North Florida Chamber Singers, see Justice Choir, "24. Resilience."

20. *The Book of Common Prayer*, 832–33.

14

Finding Hope in the Darkness of Exclusion

A Global Majority (BAME) Perspective

ROGERS GOVENDER

I RECENTLY HAD A lovely catch-up meeting on Zoom with a colleague who is a senior member of a Church-based charity with strong Human Resources links to the Church of England. They needed to recruit a new staff member and this colleague explained that she had to put up a vigorous challenge to her senior manager to not appoint the person who was deemed right for the job despite not meeting the specifications required. This was in opposition to another candidate who was excellent in interview and who met the job specifications. It was apparently clear to my colleague that the manager already knew who she wanted in the new position, even before the job was advertised! My response was that this was often my experience in the life of the church. I would suggest that this is not uncommon in church appointment processes where a Global Majority (BAME—Black, Asian, minority ethnic) candidate is invited to interview but rarely appointed to a junior or senior post.

The treatment of Global Majority people was recently raised in the news reports of the recent assault on Capitol Hill in Washington where five people lost their lives when pro-Trump supporters violently stormed the legislature. It was stated that if it was a majority Black mob the police would have reacted with stronger measures and many rioters would have possibly lost their lives. This was very obvious when compared to the Black Lives Matter protests in the wake of the murder of George Floyd in Minneapolis and elsewhere in the United States in summer 2020.

In a sermon I preached on John 1:1–14 in February 2021 at Manchester Cathedral where I serve, I suggested that the Word who became flesh and dwelt among us, the One who came as Light in the Darkness, is God who brings hope in difficult and challenging times. I suggested that there are numerous experiences of darkness in the Johannine community reflected in John's Gospel. This included the exclusion of women, the persecution and rejection and exclusion of anyone who believed in Jesus and his healing power, e.g., the blind man in John 9. Exclusion based on gender, economic background, illness, etc., is what the darkness was about. And of course there is Nicodemus, a member of the Jewish authority who comes to see Jesus in the darkness. There is the darkness of fear on the part of those who want to possibly explore a new, enlightened, liberated way. John is encouraging the church to persevere and be strong in the midst of violence, persecution, exclusion, and prejudice. He sees Jesus as the One who brings hope to their witness.

In today's social and spiritual context, I would add the exclusion and prejudice experienced by people of color and LGBTI as an experience of pain and darkness. As a priest of color with more than three decades of service in the Anglican Church, I am often cynical about racial justice and equality in God's church! Many of my LGBTI colleagues express a similar cynicism about inclusion in terms of sexuality. However, we must find encouragement from the Scriptures, from Christ who always comes as light in our darkness of exclusion, prejudice, and suffering. I would suggest that we should continue to find our hope in the living Christ in the church today.

This was my experience as a South African in the "dark" days of apartheid. We prayed for an end to apartheid. We prayed for the release of Nelson Mandela from prison. We campaigned and marched hundreds of times in our cities and towns. I did not believe I would see freedom in my lifetime! I was surprised when I heard that Mandela was to be released from Victor Verster Prison in Cape Town. On February 11, 1990, Tata Mandela walked from prison a free man! I clearly did not believe my own prayers, thanks to my growing cynicism over the years.

Theologians like Alan Boesak, Desmond Tutu, and John de Gruchy kept us on the straight and narrow of believing in hope—hope in Christ!

And by implication, hope in the witness of the church. It was De Gruchy who reminded us of Bonhoeffer's words: "Who is Jesus Christ for us today?"[1] Indeed, it was Bonhoeffer's book *The Cost of Discipleship* that helped me stay focussed in the call to be prophetic (and pastoral) in the quest for freedom, liberation, and democracy in my country of birth. Thank God for our prophets who keep challenging us to be hopeful in times of darkness. Thank God that Christ is prophet, priest, and king. Archbishop Desmond Tutu has constantly reminded us that light always overcomes darkness.

All our campaigns for racial equality and justice and the inclusion of LGBTI folks in the life of the church are based on a clear theology of inclusion. Theologians have written extensively about this and I do not intend to repeat them, except to say that I believe deeply in a theology of inclusion. I believe God is inclusive. All the words and actions of Jesus are about including and affirming people at every level of society and faith. He also has a special concern to include and affirm the "little ones":

> At that time the disciples came to Jesus, saying, "Who is the greatest in the kingdom of heaven?" And calling to him a child, he put him in the midst of them and said, "Truly, I say to you, unless you turn and become like children, you will never enter the kingdom of heaven. Whoever humbles himself like this child is the greatest in the kingdom of heaven. Whoever receives one such child in my name receives me, whoever causes one of these little ones who believe in me to sin, it would be better for him to have a great millstone fastened around his neck and to be drowned in the depth of the sea. See that you do not despise one of these little ones. For I tell you that in heaven their angels always see the face of my Father who is in heaven."[2]

Even children, who were often excluded in society, were affirmed and included by Jesus. Jesus uses rather strong terms like "be drowned in the depth of the sea" in relation to those who despise the "little ones." We know that the reference to "little ones" often refers to those who are on the edges of church and society, the "hidden" ones; the ones who are alienated and excluded.

It is usually our prejudices and fear that tend to cause us to exclude and oppress others. So, in my mature years, I am still a bit cynical. But I am also hopeful for change, for equality, and inclusion. It is our prophetic and

---

1. de Gruchy, *Theology and Ministry*, 70.
2. Matt 18:1–6, 10.

gospel imperative to be hopeful and to see Christ as our Light in the darkness of prejudice, violence, persecution, and exclusion. Let us make use of the spiritual and moral power we have in Christ to change the church and our society for the good of all God's people.

15

From Coping to Hoping

Entry into Solidarity

Thomas Hughson, SJ

Distress besets the world, the church, and all attentive persons. Creeping paralysis overtakes ordinary reflexes of thought, decision, and action on individual and social scales. We falter. Handwringing leads nowhere. Instead of catch-all answers, fear and perplexity erupt. Modern or postmodern, unbidden but importunate, the question surfaces, where is God? Has faith something to say? Where are we? What are we to do? What about myself? How do I live the spiritual life of faith amid crises of local and global magnitude? Dispersed parishes and dioceses unable to gather in full numbers, how are they to continue as worshipping communities? The COVID-19 pandemic destabilizes structures of economic cooperation and civil order no less than church polities and families with school-age children. Small businesses are shuttered. Further, in local churches as well as nation-states, polarized responses to the crises tear at social connections. Has theology something to say on behalf of faith? Who listens? And who are the "we" or "us" in the saying and listening?

Diverse geopolitical contexts—British, European, American, Asian, Middle Eastern, North or South American, for example—and alternate cultural contexts such as racial majority or minority, with or without physical disability, rural or urban, suburban or central city, economic insecurity or uninterrupted income, straight or LGBTQ—all generate different experiences. Negotiating them leads into distinct habits of mind, heart, and faith. "We" see, hear, and interpret the compounded crises in more than one way even though they affect everyone. The crises, moreover, are complex, multifaceted. Accelerating global COVID-19, international reckoning with racial oppression, with the ecological crisis of climate change, with poverty and economic instability, and divided Christian responses present multiple problems simultaneously. How can "we" cope with it all instead of letting crucial decisions to stay at home close "us" to whomever are the others? No single theological response can speak to every Christian beyond gesturing toward considerations for a conscientious perspective.

The Book of Revelation, for example, is a potent word of God. At the same time its high-octane imagery cannot but fall upon hearers and readers in very different conditions that lead to differing receptions. Some, especially in the United States where millennialism has had a protracted sway, may wonder if the global aspect of today's crises may be part of the cosmic events in the end-time. Preoccupied by concern for when the end-times are to take place, this reading can precipitate salutary fear of God and of the possibility that God's foretold judgment has actually overtaken us. If it has, then all normal, reasonable resources for problem-solving, all searching for faith and hoping for grace is beside the point. It's too late. Is that today's plight?

Christians today are not the first to be roiled by threats to their accustomed ways of life. Revelation was written when unpredictably pitiless Roman emperors controlled the externals of public life for all citizens and those simply under Roman law as conquered peoples or those like slaves not eligible for citizenship. Jews and Christians were tolerated minorities whose interior distance from emperor worship put them at frequent risk. It would seem that life described in Revelation was head-down, nose-to-the-grindstone oppression under relentless imperial power.

Imperial authority immobilized potential for citizens at large playing a formative role through public opinion; citizens obeyed and were protected by laws but enjoyed no participation in making laws. Non-citizens had little recourse. The fledgling church endured a precarious existence. Religious tolerance could be revoked in the blink of an eye. With some exceptions, Jews' and Christians' low minority status insured a subaltern Christian voice until Constantine. Imperial polity and laws smothered influence from bishops and the network of local churches from speaking on behalf of change. Paul's Letter to Philemon laid the spiritual foundation of ending slavery, at least among Christians, but local and interconnected churches had as yet no capacity to exert pressure against the institution of slavery.

The Book of Revelation's apocalyptic hope looks past human political authority to divine authority. Revelation assured that fidelity through suffering was righteous and in line with Christ's crucifixion. God's justice-charged bolts of wise heavenly interdiction will destroy the leaden weight of powers that be. Could this scenario be playing out in a new way? The visionary author dared to submit the prepossessing authority of emperors to God's overriding sovereignty and the rule of love instituted by the Lamb Who Was Slain. Revelation dethroned emperors spiritually in view of God's forthcoming earthly reign in Christ's second coming. The earliest Jewish Christians expected the imminent second coming of Christ in their lifetime.

The expectation liberated them interiorly from the overweening pressure from the cultural and political status quo. But if inward freedom was a giant step forward, what practical attitude did people take while waiting for God to change the world? Paul in 1 Thessalonians directs attention to the second coming of Christ. In the meantime some stopped working for a living. Paul teaches that if they do not work they should not expect to eat. The words of Jesus add something essential to the expectation. In Mark 13 Jesus outlines signs of the end times—upheavals in physical nature, wars, social chaos. But in Mark's telling this "little apocalypse" enjoined disciples to choices in how they lived and imagined. They were to watch like sentinels, to live according to the good news. These were acts of choice. Christians did not need to take all their cues from the powers that be because the power of God subordinates all other power and authority. Jesus was a liberator.

But the overall weight of the New Testament, particularly Luke's Gospel and Acts of the Apostles, tipped most Christians' faith toward Jesus' teaching that you know not the day nor the hour when the Lord will return like a thief in the night rather than in the midst of cosmic cataclysm. Luke challenged the early church to live, believe, think, decide, and act in the course of events with no foreseeable termination. After all, Christian faith believes with Paul in Romans 8:38–39 that nothing can separate us from the love of God poured out on us by the Holy Spirit through faith in Christ. Luke's name for God is Immanuel, God-with-us on the longer pilgrimage of history.

I would advise, consequently, that the spirit of faith today deflects concern about God's timing for the arrival of the end of history. Nonetheless, Revelation speaks to "our" powerlessness in the face of intractable suffering caused by a political regime or group. Revelation's searing divine judgment on organized human resistance to God, the poor, and believers in God remains in effect. But in that outlook there is no concept of overcoming plagues, wars, and oppression because they are seen as divine incursions.

And yet, Revelation holds an opposite message as well, one more to the point for us crisis-ridden Christians. It is blessing and support for resistance to besetting evils. The least form of resistance born of hope and trust in God is patient endurance, not letting ourselves be panicked into rash decisions and actions, or collapsing into confused stagnation. The pandemic cannot be bracketed. And patience is not a Western virtue. And yet, really, is patience all that faith can counsel us? No, only the least it can speak of. It associates our endurance of suffering with Christ's endurance of crucifixion.

Yet the cross broke the Hellenistic model of nobility in the heroic figure leading a war against a people's enemies. It departed from the Israelite profile of a Davidic warrior-king who would overthrow the Roman Empire's occupation of Israel. Jesus initiated God's kingdom along another line altogether. Isaiah's suffering servant forecast the Son of Man who came to serve not be served. The bold truth and his changing death, illness, marginalization to life, health, and fellowship upended the most powerful authorities in Israel and in the Roman occupation. Why did Christ suffer the cross for our sake? This path of God's will recedes from human comprehension, even of those who embrace it in faith. We accept it, have been saved by it, comprehend it or not, like it or not. The salvific power of Christ's passion and death according to Thomas Aquinas lay not in the pain he endured but in the love with which he underwent it. His exemplary path was one of service to others out of love for God above all and neighbor as oneself. Patient endurance of our crises leads to the crucified Christ and he takes us beyond ourselves in responding to the crises, out of unreasonable love disproportionate to any human calculus of right and wrong, injustice and justice.

Moreover, unlike the early church, contemporary crises experienced in the West are aggravated but not imposed by political power. Feints in the direction of tyranny can be seen however. By maximum contrast with abject powerlessness in early Christianity, today's entangled crises call for, and most Christians look for, beneficent human intervention. Many people across the spectrum of convictions promote positive changes. Medical research and practice, movements against racial injustice, public opinion favoring ecological culture, concern about economic equity, and constructive political measures provide avenues of hopeful thought and action. Our context allows for transitions. Revelation's spectacle of earthly tumult due to appointed angels emptying bowls of divine wrath upon proud power that oppressed the poor and the saints does not apply across the board in the West.

Where systemic racism and economic inequity dominate there Revelation counsels resistance in obedience to the creative power of God. It nowhere enjoins violent retaliation. The Book of Revelation offers inspiration and support for nonviolent action in movements on behalf of justice in today's secular spaces. Remember George Floyd. Cooperate to reduce climate change. Demand an economy that is for the people not people for the economy. Revelation encourages "our" human freedom active for justice and in seeking remedies for distorted ecological, economic, and racial structures. Revelation speaks to contemporary crises with provocative assertion of the normative implications of the superiority of divine to political authority.

Luke named God Immanuel, God-with-us. Where is Immanuel for us today? How do we find God-with-us in the midst of our confusion? Panic and perturbation steer imaginations toward rash decisions. In a contrary tendency finding God, like Job's questions directed to God, becomes the humbler question, who are we? We are created by God, set into the church by baptism, and now tried by tribulation. Even in a perilous pandemic, gratitude to God belongs to living faith. Our cries to God open us to humility freed from demands upon God that God step forward right now to change everything, to guide us in the process, and to justify to us divine tolerance of evil. Gratitude for goods not immediately threatening us overturns total preoccupation with saving ourselves from evils.

Remembering Pentecost we are called not just to benefit from salvation in Christ and whichever means others are developing toward ending the crises but also to become participants in Christ's mission and to go active. So we start to ask, how do we bear ragged, fitful witness to God-with-us? Who is God-for-us? In light of all that God has done for me, forgiving my sins, teaching and encouraging, what can I do on behalf of Christ? Baptism, confirmation, and Eucharist prompt witness—not just gladness in being a beneficiary. Ecumenical consensus holds the whole of Christianity is mis-sional and gives witness by nature. Our witness flows from and depends on the first witnesses, Christ and the Holy Spirit. How can we in different churches witness in cooperative response to this time of disturbing crises?

The "we" not only encompasses all the divided churches and ecclesial bodies but all the diverse identities people have. Not all in any classification of objective identities are cut out to be activists. Besides diversity in what may be spoken of as objective dimensions of personal identity there are also interior dimensions that are spontaneous and free. People are different. They negotiate differently the same ethnicity, gender, age, rural or urban background, economic situation, ecological conviction, level of education, sexual orientation, or political principles, etc. What about farmers, indus-trial workers, restaurant owners and employees, clergy, students, teachers, artists, lawyers, doctors, parents and grandparents, whose gifts and inter-ests differ from those encouraged by the Book of Revelation? Complement-ing the cardinal virtues of social justice and social prudence is the gift of the Holy Spirit called wisdom.

What might the Holy Spirit's gift of wisdom say in and to us? Perhaps the Spirit's gift is a twofold agenda, a paradox for us to live. On one hand we are invited to be reasonable, and on the other we are provoked to be unrea-sonable. *Ratio* means proportion. It is reasonable to disentangle the crises, their causes and effects. At the same time Christ and the Holy Spirit witness to God's obliteration of *ratio*, proportion, the reasonable, the suitable in the sending of the divine Word and Spirit. All gifts from God are dispropor-tionate to our humanity, exceed who and what we are. Living proportionate and disproportionate at the same time is our paradox. We are called to be at once reasonable believers in the gospel and to learn from God how to be unreasonable in the universal scope of our love for God and neighbor. Two of the crises—the pandemic and economic instability—are proportionate to people of good will putting their minds together in cooperative work. Faith respects and enlightens human reasoning. The pandemic and ensuing economic upheaval are susceptible to reasonable if bold solutions on the level of political life and economic initiative.

However, the ecological crisis and systemic racism are different kinds of crises. Moreover, they involve one another and the resolution for each depends on changes in self-understandings, in how "we," in this case white Christians, see ourselves. Does the "we" implied by "Western self-understandings" include racial minorities? Or are white people and white supremacy unnoticed formative influences? The crises of racism and climate change stir not a crisis of faith but rather a crisis of charity. How unreasonable can love be? Can whites let go of entrenched white supremacy and satisfaction with reaping the harvest of the world's resources? These challenges fall into the new perspective of charity and a calling to be as unreasonable in love as Christ is.

The contemporary mode of charity involves global human solidarity as the underlying positive ground being thrown into relief by global crises. "We" are being invited as seldom before to global acknowledgement of human solidarity marked not by uniformity but by attention to the open-ended diversity in who "we" are. The "we" in suffering human solidarity forces a choice between enclosure in our closest already-established identity and self-transcending into a "we" of many identities of diverse people, groups, and nations. We encounter an unreasonable invitation of divine love in the face of great challenges. Faith says to us amid our crises "sustain and develop solidarity."

16

Siblinghood Between Those with Super-Yachts and Those with Just One Oar

The Hope of a Celebration of Ethnic Diversity in the Church of England

SHEMIL MATHEW

> We are not all in the same boat. We are all in the same storm.
> Some are on super-yachts. Some have just the one oar.
>
> —DAMIAN BARR

I AM WRITING THIS during the second peak of the COVID-19 pandemic. As with most crises, we have seen the altruistic spirit of humanity shining through the darkness we find ourselves in. However, it can also be said our awareness of the social, racial, and economic unevenness of our society in the United Kingdom has never been as acute as it is now. Damian Barr's words point towards the hypocrisy of our society, which often responds to the fact that COVID-19 affects some communities more than others with the line that we are all in the same boat. This is the same attitude that responds to the Black Lives Matter movement with the retort that all life matters. Barr reminds us that there is no compassion in generalizing or gaslighting someone's suffering: a truly compassionate response is to accept and work against the inequalities in our society.

I am an ordained priest of the Church of England, currently working as a university chaplain and theological educator. I am also researching two diaspora Anglican communities from the southern Indian state of Kerala in England and their relationship with the Church of England for my PhD. This chapter is a reflection on my journey so far. I will start with a story from my childhood as a backdrop, then I will go on to reflect on my journey of discerning vocations and circumstances leading to the founding of Anglican Minority Ethnic Network (AMEN). Just like many other stories in which we hear about the struggles of minority communities, this is a story of struggle and gathering the courage to stand up against the overpowering, oppressive majority. The final two sections of this chapter will suggest where hope may be found: not in homogeneity, but an interconnected diversity.

A Sea with Many Boats

Let me begin by sharing an experience from my childhood growing up in Kerala.

"My father says you are rice Christians!" shouted an elder cousin to six-year-old me and my brother, my first introduction to my identity as a global Anglican Christian. Let me give you some context. It had been a very exciting day. It was the day of our quinquennial family gathering, the first one I remember. Around two thousand of our extended family had gathered to reacquaint ourselves with our relatives and to teach the younger generation of the proud family story that goes back many centuries to the time of Saint Thomas the Apostle, believed to have arrived sometime in the first century, converting a number of high caste Hindu families.

Colonial explorers were amazed and perhaps even perplexed by the deeply established Christian tradition in Kerala. Despite limited contact with Christianity around the world (other than limited contact with the church in Antioch) and its struggle to survive as a minority church, the Indian Church at the time of colonial expansion had almost 1,700 years of history, liturgical traditions, and a place in the caste hierarchy of the land. Our *Ammachies* (grandmas) often told us the story of *Koonan Kurishu Sathyam*. This story narrated the events of 1653 when, in response to the Portuguese attempts to bring the Indian Church under the Pope, our ancestors held on to a rope that was tied to the cross on top of the church and swore an oath rejecting everything that comes from Rome and the Pope.

The Portuguese were followed by the Dutch, then the British. With the inauguration of the modern missionary movement, Catholic missionaries were replaced by an even bigger number of Protestant missionaries. The peculiarity of missions in Kerala was that they weren't established to convert people of other religions; rather, their role was to convert the ancient Christians of Kerala. Early Church Missionary Society (CMS—an Anglican missionary agency now based in Oxford, England) records and letters ooze with confidence that the local church (despite its much older heritage and liturgy) would convert to the Anglican faith once they had learned the true gospel.

My cousin's comment about being a "rice Christian" alluded to the fact that my great-grandfather left the ancestral church to join the Anglicans during the colonial period. Those who joined the Anglican Church found themselves favored by the colonial government and establishment. The phrase clearly implied that we are descendants of those who betrayed the ancestral faith in search of economic advantage, i.e., to ensure a steady supply of rice on the dinner table. Even at that age, I knew that this was not a baseless accusation. After all, I was studying at the CMS school. My father was a professor at the CMS college, my grandfather had been a tea planter in the English tea plantation, and my great grandfather had been a schoolteacher in the local CMS school.

Discernment When You Are in the Sea with Just an Oar

I started exploring a calling to priestly ministry as a young person within my home diocese. At that time, the advice was to get a theological education overseas and then return. Having studied overseas, I continued a vocational conversation with the Church of Ceylon, where I was working with CMS. The conversation was encouraging, but the diocese, quite understandably, needed a longer time commitment. On my return to the United Kingdom at the conclusion of our work contract, I began again with the DDO (Diocesan Director of Ordinands—in charge of guiding those in my position) in the English diocese where we were based on home leave. It became very clear early on that my journey into Anglican vocations was going to be different from the one I had read about in books and blogs. I was now married to a Church of England priest and she shared with me her experiences with the vocations team. Despite having a very strong academic background with degrees in English literature and theology at both undergraduate and postgraduate level, I suspect I had neither the courage nor the right vocabulary to articulate my struggle going through discernment at that stage.

The first stage for any ordinand is to realize that there are many gatekeepers along the way: parish priests, vocations advisors, DDOs, diocesan vocations advisors, bishops, bishops' advisors—each and all of them hold power over this journey. As the word gatekeeper implies, it is indeed their role to watch over and ensure that the right people go in and the wrong people stay out. Under this regime, the overall feeling of an ordinand going through the discernment process is one of helplessness: boats that gave you comfort and confidence, such as previous jobs and your home, are taken away from under you; if you are entering residential training at a theological college, then you might feel that your boat has been substituted with a rubber dinghy and that your dinghy is just one amongst many others. But if you are "different"—in your sexual orientation or ethnic identity, for example—then you may also find that you don't even have an oar to help you navigate the shark-infested waters.

In my case, as a cradle Anglican with the experience of working within the Church of England and the wider Anglican Communion, I was at first amused, then annoyed when I was informed that I lacked experience of the Anglican Church and would therefore not be considered for a BAP (Bishop's Advisory Panel—the final round of interviews before being admitted for ordination training). In response to this, I requested a meeting with the DDO: I had to wait nine months for an appointment.

Further along my journey, I began to notice multiple instances of what I now consider to have been racial micro-aggressions and even clear attempts to block my vocational journey. I have forgotten the number of times I was asked "Where you are from?" In this context, the question was particularly loaded, as those asking would have already read my files, known whereabouts in the diocese I lived, who I was married to, and what my heritage is. Later, I realized it was a tool of oppression used to put me in the "rightful" position of a foreigner, not a sibling. This was death by a thousand cuts: a process of being undervalued and reminded constantly that you are not the same. This was the exact opposite of what is intended in the Anglican formation process, which is to provide competent and confident leadership for the church of tomorrow.

Anglican Minority Ethnic Network—A Dunkirk Moment in My Vocations

Damian Barr's lines remind us of the different vessels that navigate tumultuous seas. Personally, I am reminded of what has come to be known as the Dunkirk miracle of 1940. This was truly a moment where British bravery and ingenuity came into its own. The flotilla of hundreds of little ships at Dunkirk not only saved the lives of 338,226 young men trapped between the English Channel and the advancing German army, it also changed the course of the Second World War. These little ships were successful because of their small size, not despite it. It was because they were small that they managed to get closer to the shore than the big ships could and thereby rescue as many people as possible.

My Dunkirk moment came when I met other ordinands from different minority ethnic backgrounds. I soon realized that my vision was shared particularly by an ordinand of Portuguese heritage, Joseph Fernandes. We started meeting with each other and thought about what we could do to help those who were going through the discernment process as well as those who are in training. However, we knew that as two ordinands at the bottom of the pecking order of a hierarchical structure, we could do very little. Even if we tied our rubber dinghies together, we were still without an oar. Thankfully, at that moment we were given help and assistance in the form of our very supportive theological college principal, the Very Revd. Professor Martyn Percy. Accepting the risks, he offered us both the financial and moral support to organize a national conference in 2014. At this point, more super-yachts came to help, such as the then-national advisor for the Committee for Minority Ethnic Anglican Concerns, Dr. Elizabeth Henry. This national conference marked the tying of our boats together, followed by many meetings on a Facebook group. A year later, AMEN CofE (Church of England) merged with a bigger organization called Latimer Group in the leadership of Revd. Dr. Chigor Chike and Revd. Taemin Oh. Fast forward to 2021 and we can say that we continued on the path of connecting people and networking with over 150 subscribed members and over five hundred people in the Facebook group.

My own continuing journey showed that the struggle does not end with the conclusion of the training period: finding a curacy came with fresh challenges. By this time, I was in the final stages of completing an MTh with the University of Oxford and still teaching ordinands at another Church of

England institution. I was officially told that my sending diocese did not have a suitable curacy for me. Unofficially, I was told that the parish did not think my English was up to scratch. At the same time, my wife—who was serving as a priest in the same diocese—was eight months pregnant and about to begin maternity leave. We were told the best the diocese could offer was a non-stipendiary curacy (unpaid post). The message from senior leadership was that if you get any better offer from elsewhere then please take it. AMEN did offer pastoral support, but as we are a flotilla of rubber dinghies and not super-yachts, the help offered was limited.

This is a lesson that has become increasingly clear in the last seven years working with AMEN: the idea that minority ethnic people look for help from other minority ethnic people is a worthy principle but—at present—it does not work well enough in practice. First of all, minority ethnic people are diverse: often, the only thing connecting them is the fact that they are all part of the Church of England. Second, even if we are ready to forego our internal differences, we need to acknowledge that a minority in the overall population will command little power over the majority. Third and above all, centuries of institutional racism and only very recent, tepid encouragement of a diverse leadership ensures that the Church of England does not have a representative number of minority ethnic senior clergy or lay people. Super-yachts need to help rubber dinghies, but this is only possible if the super-yachts realize they are inherently privileged by their skin color, their education, and their social and ecclesiological status.

In recent months, the term white privilege has gained some attention and is often misinterpreted. The "white" in white privilege does not signify skin tone. Of course, there are many tones of whiteness and socioeconomic disparities among white people. Rather, white privilege implies that a group of people who are not considered white (in all shades of yellow, brown and black) are discriminated against. In other words, just like darkness is the absence of light, whiteness is the absence of being discriminated against on racial grounds. At one level this is not having the p- or n-word shouted at you in the street, or not having to worry that you might not get the medical treatment or job you need, or not having to worry about sending your children to particular schools or clubs. A much deeper and more dangerous side to white privilege is that even though the majority world population is not considered "white," the "white" body is often seen as the norm. This may be an inconvenience when Zoom virtual backgrounds struggle to identify your face, but it could be fatal when pulse oximeters and thermometers constantly make error readings for those who are not white.

To return to my predicament in searching for a curacy, though, help did come in the end. It was the theological college principal, the first super-yacht, who introduced me to a different diocese and a compassionate DDO, which lead to a wonderful curacy under an experienced priest who modeled a humble, effective ministry. With the waves they make, these super-yachts could have easily wiped out my humble rubber dinghy and thrown me overboard, but instead they used their privilege to lift me up.

Hope: A Siblinghood of Boats of Many Sizes!

What hurt most about my cousin's "rice Christians" comment was that it divided us after a day of unity. Siblinghood is different from and more complex than any other relationship one may have: we can choose our friends but we cannot choose family. Siblings will be part of our lives whether we like them or not. Unlike our parents, who may leave us, and children, who may join us, siblings will be with us for most or even all of our lives. Acknowledging the complexity of the relationship between siblings, the Bible contains a string of stories about sibling relationships and rivalry. In the opening chapters, we see the first siblings: although united by their bloodline, they are inherently different. Their difference leads to the elder brother Cain becoming envious of and in the end murdering Abel. Siblinghood does not mean that we are all the same; it means that we share a common human family but we will continue to be different.

I accept that a vague understanding of the siblinghood of humanity has always been present in Western church and academy. Monogenesis (the teaching that all humanity came to be from the same ancestral parents) has been an accepted teaching for the church. The sacrament of the Eucharist at the heart of any church community is a celebration of this common humanity; we are reminded at the Eucharistic service of the words of Saint Paul: "Because there is one bread, we who are many are one body, for we all partake of the one bread" (1 Cor 10:17). However, the reality of human experience is that we have always tried to establish a hierarchy in our siblinghood, just as sibling rivalry is a constant theme in the Old Testament. In history we have witnessed the church using the story of the curse of Ham in Genesis 9:20–27 to justify one of the worst human transgressions of all time—the transatlantic slave trade. Hundreds of thousands of human beings were transported in slave ships like worms. The greed of a rapidly industrializing society was not the only culprit here: the church deemed the black race as cursed to be servants to the other people groups. Pseudoscientific race categories developed by Johann Friedrich Blumenbach in the eighteenth century still form our understanding of race categories and racial difference. More than two hundred years later, with modern research proving that we are but a single species, our judgment and thinking is still clouded by Blumenbach's race categories. Every genocide in modern history has begun with one group denying another group's humanity; when we even think that people of a different race are less than human we are denying their humanity, we are denying their right to live.

There is a need for our country and church to continue to repent of its sins of racism and slave trading in the past. This need arises not from the need to install a feeling of white guilt in descendants of oppressors, but out of the realization that past oppression still affects people today. The transatlantic slave trade was not just forcing one group of people to work for another group of people; it was the systematic destruction of an entire people group, stripping them of their cultures, languages, families and communities. Such widespread and organized abuse affects not just one generation but carries on in ripples, affecting the many that came after. Continued racism in Western society, which prevents minority ethnic people from accessing education and healthcare, adds power to those ripples, often building them into waves of injustice.

In these times, I believe that the hope for the Church of England and its relationship with minority ethnic communities also lies in people who themselves identify as minority ethnic rising up as prophetic voices. The biblical tradition of prophets is that of challenging oppression and injustice even to the point of martyrdom. Minority ethnic communities must use their experience of being different and being a minority as a strength, and not succumb to a deeply paralyzing feeling of victimhood. This is what Jesus meant when he asked his disciples to be the salt of the earth—to be a transformative and preserving influence.

Networks such as AMEN can be a source of hope for both the Church of England and its minority ethnic communities, because they bring many rubber dinghies—with their prophetic voices—together. This is the reason why, from the very early days, we decided that AMEN membership is open to anyone, regardless of skin color or self-identification with a minority or a majority ethnicity. For us, this is an acceptance of our siblinghood, of our common humanity as children of God.

From my own perspective and experience, I can see that super-yachts may be able to save some dinghies and guide them to the right place. However, this can only happen if we nourish a culture that teaches the truth about the injustices inherent in our society. Only if we go through a process of reconciliation and forgiveness will the super-yachts of the Church of England be able to slow down and develop a humbler theology. This requires accepting our past sins and finding the path of true repentance, turning away from what went wrong and ensuring such wrongs never happen again by fighting against injustice. To return to the Dunkirk analogy, we ought to remember that retreat was not the end of the war; rather, it was the beginning of a process that led to many of those rescued soldiers—with much reinforcement from stronger ships and greater stores of ammunition—returning to the beaches of Normandy. Fighting for justice is perhaps another step beyond our comfort zone, further out even than being prophetic voices. We don't just need the rubber dinghies and super-yachts; we need all our ammunition for this fight.

In the context of the Church of England, this fight includes exposing racism in our institution, campaigning for more ethnic diversity in the senior leadership, making strategic alliances to elect more minority ethnic people to bodies all the way from general synod down to parish councils. We must make our churches welcoming and open to the participation of people from our diverse communities, we must challenge and change our liturgy so that it may reflect diversity and support inclusion and participation. Only once we begin this fight, once we begin to accept that we are all siblings, will we also start to truly reflect the church as it should be, the eschatological worshiping community formed of people from all tribes, nations, and languages (Rev 7:9).

17

The Scandal of Being Human
in a Time of Pandemic!

ALAN JONES

ONE OF THE MOST radical and scandalous teachings of our tradition is that
God has created us neighbors. We were made for communion and connection. It sounds simple and straightforward but history is one long messy
story of our failure to be true neighbors. Our common humanity, such as it
is, is frayed and stretched by uncertainty and ambiguity, by each of us being
an instance of wild improbability struggling for meaning and purpose. The
pandemic of injustice raises the question, what kind of creatures are we?
What makes us tick? How should we relate to each other?

> Jesus was asked:
> "Teacher, which is the greatest commandment in the Law?"
> He replied: "'Love the Lord your God with all your heart and with
> all your soul and with all your mind.' This is the first and great-
> est commandment. And the second is like it: 'Love your neigh-
> bor as yourself.' All the Law and the Prophets hang on these two
> commandments."[1]

"And who is my neighbor?" The answer that Jesus gave was a parable,
commonly called "The Parable of the Good Samaritan" (Luke 10:30–37).
In the story, a Jewish traveler is beaten, robbed, and left half dead along
the road. First a priest and then a Levite pass by, but both avoid the man.

---

1. Matt 22:36–40 (NIV).

Finally, a Samaritan sees the man lying in the road and he helps him, not only binding up his wounds and taking him to an inn but also paying his expenses. The important thing to remember is that Samaritans and Jews despised each other. We might rename the parable by referring to any group we fear or hate—"The Parable of the Good Muslim" or "The Parable of the Good Republican/Democrat," "The Parable of the Good Liberal/Tea Party Candidate," or "The Parable of the Black/White Politician." The shocking truth is that God created us neighbors.

In 1849 in Vienna Salomon Mosenthal wrote a play called *Deborah*—foreseeing the time, he wrote, when "the Christian and the Jew will become human beings." Being a true neighbor to each other is the way to become truly human. Exploring what it is to be human is our Common Ground. Now, over a hundred and sixty years after Mosenthal wrote his play, we are still waiting for the Christians and the Jews, the Muslims, the Hindus, the Buddhists—the whole panoply of religious traditions along with atheists and agnostics—to become human beings.

The great religious traditions, at their best, tell us that the fundamental scandal of being human is that we are all related. *We are neighbors.* I cannot be me without you. You cannot be you without me. Not me without you. Not you without me.

Why is this a scandal? A scandal is something that trips us up—a stumbling block. Religion tends to be scandalous in several ways: first, by reason of the sometimes terrible behavior of its adherents. Often its claim to absolute and ultimate truth sounds scandalous. It is also scandalous—it trips us up—by claiming that there's a breathtaking charity at the heart of things. So, the question is, "When will we become human beings?" God created us neighbors. When will we get with the program?

We get to the heart of things by storytelling. One of the great things I admire about Judaism is that the God we claim to worship cannot ultimately be caught in language. God cannot be said or spoken. The divine is unsayable. This is why stories are important. They say something, but, if they are good stories, they are open to endless interpretation.

The world festers with the raucous certainties of politics, ideology, and religion, and the self-serving stories that support them. Saint John of the Cross cuts through the lies with a maxim: "*In the end we shall be examined in love.*" That's it. That's the test of any religion; the test of atheism. It's the test of being human. *God created us neighbors and in the end we shall be examined in love.* But most of us most of the time cannot stand the ambiguity, uncertainty, and amazement that being human entails. That's why we are attracted by what we think of as hard facts. We don't like open-ended stories. Endless interpretation is unendurable.

How to solve the problem? We say something like, "Let's cut through the ambiguity and uncertainty and get to the facts." Religious people got into trouble when they tried—about three hundred years ago—to do just that. They began to treat religion as if it were like science—an *explanation* of how God runs the world. Facts were front and center. Stories were merely backup. When religion sets itself up as if it were a scientific explanation of the world, it looks increasingly ridiculous, particularly when the "facts" are about a pandemic. Religion is about storytelling and storytelling brings with it a whole host of problems. The famous Marxist dictum that religion is "the opiate of the people" speaks to the need for a comforting, justifying, all-encompassing narrative. We need stories as a kind of drug to provide us with the illusion that things make sense. That's why storytelling can be dangerous. And when a story gets in our blood we tend to take it literally and deny the possibility of *other* stories and *other* interpretations. Our politics are about competing stories as to the true nature of being human and the vocation of America.

The quest for meaning acts as a drug. We're all looking for a narrative, a story to make sense of things. Mere information isn't enough. Our love of stories, novels, movies, adventures, science fiction, romance, horror, sit-coms, gossip is understandable. They play an important part in helping us interpret the world and simply get through the day. They provide the architecture of our thoughts and feelings. They tell us who our tribal neighbors are—what it means to be Jewish, Christian, Muslim, American, atheist, black, gay, female. And our stories aren't in sync—they don't mesh. There's nothing more unnerving than to discover yourself in an unflattering role in someone else's story. Perhaps, the role of villain or persecutor, or worse, the role of someone barely visible—a nobody. This is where I find the Jewish tradition of interpretation of stories not only helpful but a lifeline. The rabbinic method of endless argument is truly a lifesaver. But "endless argument" presupposes a strong community of trust where we can disagree—sometimes heatedly—without breaking the bonds of the community.

So, let's take a brief look at the great story of Moses. He is, after all, very much part of the American Story.[2] From Plymouth Rock onwards,

2. Feiler, *America's Prophet.*

the early settlers saw Moses as central to the American experiment. The revolutionaries, the slaves, *and* the slaveholders—all saw themselves as people of the Exodus. The slaveholders had thrown off the yoke of Europe and its monarchies and had entered the promised land. The slaves were still in Egypt and sang "Let my people go!" The Jordan was the Ohio River.

Deuteronomy was the biblical book most often quoted during the founding era. Two themes again: the Exodus—the call to freedom—*and* the restraint of divine law—the call to obedience. Both are aspects of what it means to be neighbors of and to each other. Alas, at the heart of our foundation as a people is a deep and vile betrayal of the great biblical principle: *God created us neighbors.* We tend to be more concerned with who's in and who's out—with rules of exclusion rather than the vision of one people.

We are neighbors. That's who we are. It is how we are constituted. That's why we must be open to the revision of our stories and repudiate the lies and distortions often embedded in them.

One way we fight our amnesia and cynicism is to have public rituals of remembrance. In Germany a *Memorial Day for the Victims of National Socialism* is indeed an appropriate response—if not an atonement—for crimes committed. I wonder what would happen if England had a *Refusal to Grant Refugee Jews Asylum Memorial Day*, or an *Incendiary Bombing of German Cities Memorial Day*, or—casting the shadow forward here in the United States—what would happen if we had an *Iraqi Civilians Memorial Day* or *A Children Living in Poverty Day*? It's hard for us to remember—since God created us neighbors—how we have betrayed our own flesh and blood. Our stories remind us that we are mortal and that there are inexorable limits to our power. The good news is that a culture that has become aware of these limits will turn at some point to the effort to recover the sacred. This is not the rediscovery of a cloying piety but a glimpse of the terror and wonder of being alive at all and our common journey from cradle to grave. And a central part of rediscovering the sacred is rediscovering that we're in this together. We are neighbors in the context of the awesome mystery of God.

I believe the recovery of the sacred—the ground of our common humanity—is the central spiritual task of our day. It fuels our passion for justice and our care for the environment. It shows up just how naïve and irresponsible it is to think that secularism is benign and religion is not. The "new" atheists underestimate the undertow of nihilism.

The planet itself is answering back, demanding a recovery of the sense of the sacred. The degraded environment is rising up. What we used to call the "natural world" (from which we think we escape) is making a spectacular comeback. Haven't we come to the end of thinking that technology will solve *all* our problems? Hasn't the *story* of unlimited progress become discredited? We don't think of ourselves as neighbors. We are autonomous isolated individuals, stabbing at a virtual and phony internet intimacy. We are *consumers* bent on acquisitiveness. Consumers don't make good citizens. "God" becomes a scandal by being a big ugly toy that rival gangs of children fight over; or by becoming an object of ridicule for those who have grown up and out of such childish things. Or could God be a sign of the struggle to live into what it might mean to be human? Without a sense of the sacred, we lose touch with the sources of the very values we take for granted—the dignity of the human person, the rule of law, human rights. Without a sense of the sacred, we become idiots and it's time for all of us to stop being idiots and to become neighbors.

In Greek and Latin, "idiot" means a "private person": that is someone caught up in a private world of self-preservation and safety with no regard for the common good or obligations of citizenship. The word "idiot" was used derisively in ancient Athens to refer to one who declined to take part in public life. We are a nation of idiots and our idiocy leads to polarization and violence, to possible death by stupidity. We like it that way. We confuse this "idiocy" with freedom. It's a scandal. It's its own form of nihilism—a story that ends not with a bang but a whimper. Idiocy (in this ancient sense) makes is difficult for us to talk to each other, and when we do it's at cross-purposes. This isn't to say that there isn't a lot of noise in the public square, but few are actually listening and speaking to each other. We live mainly in a world of private citizens screaming their frustrations publicly.

I want to affirm a story, which tells us that far more things bind us together—atheists, believers, and all those in between—than anything that tears us apart. If we're awake to the wonders of modern science—the vastness of the universe, the sheer time-scale of creation—we realize we are all bound together by amazement, uncertainty, and humility. We are all bound together by the sacred.

The good news is there's more going on than my little psychodrama. And if we don't find a creative outlet for our longings, there are plenty of destructive "solutions" in religion and ideology. It's no accident that people, longing for something to count on and trust, feel drawn to authoritarianism in both politics and religion.

What can spring us out of the idiotic prison of the merely private and rancidly individualistic? Circumstances can jolt us out of our present position. Many are feeling the pain of dislocation, unemployment, loss of home, as well as the inner miseries of depression and addiction. There's a lot to be depressed and worried about. Given the challenges facing us, we need a new conversation—a new story about our being created neighbors. The noble words used to describe our highest aspirations and longings—words like "freedom," "dignity," "virtue"—have been corrupted. They become codewords. Freedom = the right to carry a gun; dignity = the right to think of ourselves as autonomous, with no reference to the needs of others—the right to be idiots; virtue = the fantasy that we are the truly righteous, while others are deeply wicked. But our romance with rugged individualism is coming to an end. Tocqueville used the word *individualisme* unflatteringly. It was a word to describe the terrible atomizing forces let loose by the French Revolution. Americans quickly gave it "an almost entirely sunny sense. It was no longer a dark force that needed correction from outside, one crushing public virtue, but was itself the source of all American virtue."[3] Gary Wills comments, "It [individualism] was ideologically unchallengeable. Opposing individualism became unpatriotic. It was identified with the frontier values, with the free market, with freedom itself."[4]

Our confusing freedom with a sunny individualism is why we're strangely schizophrenic politically. Idiots. On the one hand, we want no infringement of our private freedoms and at the same time we want to be protected from social fragmentation, epidemic violence, and economic and technological change—always accelerating faster than our ability to absorb it. Our appetites undermine the very values we espouse. We don't want "socialized" medicine but we love Medicare. We don't want to be the world's policeman yet we think we know what's good for the rest of humanity.

Our shallow and "idiotic" view of freedom, ironically, pushes us deeper into our home-grown slaveries—slavery to our appetites and "rights," slavery to our addictions and our "freedom" to go to hell any way we damn well choose. We are caught in the worst story of all in which, as acquisitive consumers, we are natural enemies of each other.

So . . . let's not be deceived because the word "neighbor" sounds bland. We are called to be *kind* to one another. When, decades ago, Huston Smith asked Aldous Huxley if he had any regrets, he said, "Yes. I wish I had been

3. Wills, *Head and Heart*, 79.
4. Wills, *Head and Heart*, 81.

more kind." In its earlier use the word was much stronger. The fourteenth-century mystic Julian of Norwich wrote, "God is kind in his being." It meant benevolence of course, but also the word reflected the nature of a thing—of what *kind* it was. And finally, the word is connected to kin and kindred. So, to say that someone treated you "kindly" would be to say that he or she acted in a benevolent way (kindly), as if you were a relative (kindred), and in a way that is only natural to someone like him or her (his or her kind). Julian saw that the world is full of "unkyndnesse." So, the question is, "What kind of people are we?" Do we understand our true nature as neighbors?

Remember Salomon Mosenthal who in 1849 foresaw the time when "the Christian and the Jew will become human beings"? Now the vision includes the whole human family. It has been a long journey—and it is far from over. The scandal is that God created us *neighbors*. Our obligation isn't to diagnose but to love each other—while there is still time. In the end, we shall be examined in love.

18

COVID-19 and Inequalities in Health

The Relevance of Liberation Theology

SARAH COTES

COVID-19 HAS SHONE A searchlight on our society and the links between poverty and ill health. In this essay I discuss these links as they exist in England, a rich nation. Others have shown that the same links are equally clear in other rich nations, notably the United States, where inequalities are even greater. I have drawn heavily on work led by Sir Michael Marmot, from which Figures 1, 3–5 are drawn.[1] I show that the inequalities of health and wealth in England reveal oppression of the poor and vulnerable, and hence an appropriate background against which the principles of liberation theology should be applied.

COVID-19 emerged in the United Kingdom at the beginning of March 2020. It was soon clear that the disease had a higher incidence and mortality among the poor. Frontline health workers, many of whom are paid low wages, and from ethnic minorities, were also affected disproportionately. They entered the public consciousness as the moral backbone of the nation, risking their lives on behalf of others. The disproportionate death rate

1 See Marmot et al., "Health Equity in England." The figures in this essay are taken with permission from the review.

122

from COVID-19 among Black, Asian, and minority ethnic (BAME) groups raised awareness of persistent racism in our society.[2]

The pandemic has confronted us with the extent of poverty in the United Kingdom, officially defined as a household income less than 60 percent of the median. By this definition, after housing costs are deducted, 22 percent of the population live in poverty, including 30 percent of children.[3] Some see employment as the way out of poverty (and it can be). But statistics show that, although employment has risen in the United Kingdom, wages are often so low that poverty exists among 10 percent of working households, and 70 percent of children in poverty are living in working households. But is this *real* poverty? The above measure is a relative one. One measure of real poverty is whether the poor can afford to eat an adequate diet. The food banks confirm that we do have a problem—their use has become normalized and in the last five years has increased by 128 percent.[4] If people cannot afford adequate food we are right to say there is real poverty. Further evidence has confirmed the National Health Service–recommended diet is quite unaffordable for those on a low income.[5]

People debate the causes of poverty. It is commonly attributed to indolence ("skivers"), ignorance, or malice ("benefit cheats"). Only 3.9 percent of claims in the United Kingdom were thought to be due to fraud or error (not separately identified) in 2020–21.[6] But people in work who are not indolent remain poor. Some have seen the cause of poverty as economic lag, and that the solution would be a trickle-down of wealth. This theory was championed by Margaret Thatcher and Ronald Reagan but is no longer accepted. Off-shore tax havens have flourished instead. Others believe that poverty has a structural basis – the way society is organized or governed. Figure 1 shows the distribution of deprivation across England by Index of Multiple Deprivation (IMD)[7]—an index that takes account of income, employment, housing, health, crime rate, education, and living environment. .Such regional disparity is likely to have a structural cause.

2. Public Health England, "Disparities in the Risk."

3. "Poverty in the UK," 2.1, 2.2.

4. "End of Year Stats," fig. 1.

5. See "Hungry for Change," para. 54, and Scott et al., "Affordability of the UK's Eatwell Guide."

6. See "Fraud and Error in the Benefit System," para. 1.

7. "English Indices of Deprivation 2019."

Figure 1—Distribution of the Index of Multiple Deprivation (IMD) 2019 by local authority based on the proportion of neighborhoods in the most deprived deciles nationally

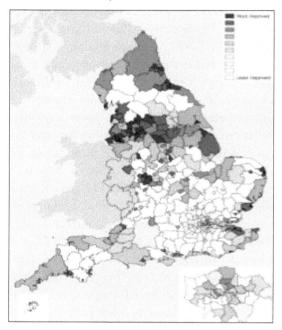

In the poorest countries life expectancy relates to the national income per person. In the early stages of national development, the death rate falls as income rises to a point above which, in richer countries, life expectancy ceases to rise in parallel with the national income (it may rise slowly for other reasons). Mortality in richer countries (including the United Kingdom and the United States) then relates to socioeconomic gradient—the distribution of wealth within that particular society.[8] In England there is a seven-year difference in life expectancy and a seventeen-year difference in disability-free life between the lowest and highest socioeconomic deciles in the population (Figure 2).[9] The higher rates of mortality and disability among the more deprived raises the overall mortality.

8. Wilkinson and Pickett, *Spirit Leve*, 18–23.
9. White and Butt, "Inequality in Health and Life Expectancies," figure 2.

Figure 2—Life expectancy and disability-free life expectancy (DFLE) at birth (males), persons by neighborhood income level, England, 1999–2003.

Note: Each dot represents life expectancy (LE) or disability-free life expectancy (DFLE) of a neighborhood (middle level—super output area).

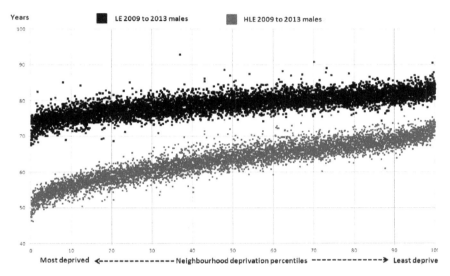

The graph for females shows a similar gradient with slightly longer life expectancy.

Do unhealthy people just drift to the bottom? Social mobility may indeed explain to some extent why the unhealthy accumulate in the lower socioeconomic deciles but cannot explain the higher prevalence *overall* of ill health in more unequal societies. Some blame health inequalities on lifestyle choices, but Marmot maintains one has to look at the "causes of the causes" of ill health. He highlights the complex interactions between the various components of deprivation—income, education, environment, employment opportunities, housing, and intergenerational influences. Furthermore, people cannot avoid comparing themselves to others, and poorer people acquire a sense of failure and low self-esteem. In a seminal study of civil servants, Marmot observed a marked social gradient in the incidence of coronary heart disease.[10] He controlled for all the usual risk factors (smoking, obesity, level of activity, blood pressure, and cholesterol) and found the incidence of coronary heart disease correlated most strongly

10. Marmot et al., "Contribution of Job Control."

with the degree of control subjects had over their work. He also found that mental health showed a marked social gradient in this group and a higher incidence of suicide among the more deprived. Known biological and psychological mechanisms related to stress can lead to smoking, alcohol abuse, and excess eating. The relationship between all these drivers of ill health are complex, but links to socio-economic gradient are clear.

The higher rates of illness and death among BAME groups (for some groups double that in white people) are partially explained by greater poverty in those groups. They are also more likely to live in multi-generational housing and show a higher incidence of obesity, hypertension, and diabetes, all factors linked to mortality from COVID-19. This does not explain *why* these illnesses are more prevalent among these groups. It is unlikely to be genetic as they comprise many different ethnicities. In the light of Marmot's work (above) I suggest that the additional stress of living as members of a racial minority may be a factor. More research is needed.

Marmot showed in 2020 that by most criteria inequalities have increased since 2010. Unemployment has fallen, but wages have fallen and in-work poverty has increased. He summarizes the effect of inequality on the "avoidable causes of mortality" in Figure 3.[11] He notes also that the annual increase in life expectancy seen in the past has stalled and for some groups has fallen. He finds no explanation for this other than the policy of austerity in recent years—a political choice, since not all countries chose this and some did better for not choosing it.[12] Austerity has caused loss of life on a large scale.

Figure 3—Age standardized avoidable mortality rates (per 100,000) by decile of deprivation in England, 2017.

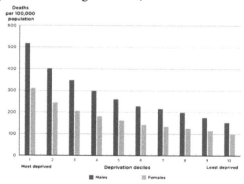

11. "Socio-economic Inequalities in Avoidable Mortality."

12. Stuckler and Basu, *Body Economic.*

Can poor health be blamed on the individual? Tony Blair, when Prime Minister, said that health problems were "questions of individual lifestyle—obesity, smoking, alcohol abuse, diabetes, sexually transmitted disease . . . the result of millions of individual decisions."[13] Individual decisions do matter. Lack of exercise, for example, contributes to obesity. But when there is no work, no money for a gym club, and green spaces are less congenial, exercise is less enjoyable. I have already discussed the unaffordability of a healthy diet for some. Furthermore, people forced to work for economic reasons may not have time or energy to cook, and instead buy convenience foods. The causes of obesity are multifactorial; what is clear is the link between inequality and obesity.[14] In short, the data do not support Tony Blair's view.

Do the poverty and inequality we see amount to oppression? If so, by whom or what are people oppressed? The effects of inequality have been known since "The Black Report" in 1980.[15] This report particularly commented on the unequal provision of health care. In 2010 Marmot made recommendations for addressing health inequalities. These were mainly accepted by David Cameron's government. The issues were, therefore, recognized. Even so, since 2010 government spending has fallen. Large cuts to the budgets of local authorities (responsible for public health) have impacted most on the areas of greatest deprivation (Figure 4).[16] Marmot adds the effect of tax and benefit changes (Figure 5).[17] It is shockingly apparent that the most deprived have suffered the greatest reduction in income, especially those of working age with children. Inescapably, this is injustice and oppression of the poor and vulnerable.

13. "Blair Calls for Lifestyle Change," paras. 15–16.
14. Schrecker and Bambra, *How Politics Makes Us Sick*, 29–41.
15. See "Black Report 1980."
16. See also Phillips and Simpson, "Changes in Councils' Adult Social Care."
17. See also Hood and Waters, "Impact of Tax and Benefit Reforms."

Figure 4—Average change in council service spending per person by quintile of Index of Multiple Deprivation (IMD), average score, 2009/10 to 2017/18. Displays spending on adult social care (ASC), total local authority (LA) spending, and other services.

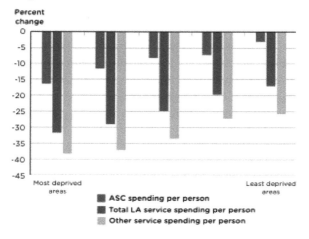

Figure 5—Long-run impact of planned tax and benefit reforms by income decile and household type, UK, May 2015–June 2017.

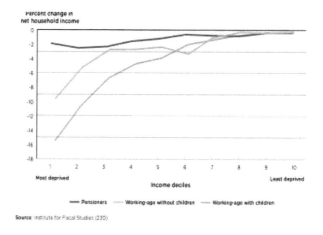

Acceptance of inequality and its associated harm, if it does not derive from callousness, derives from the neoliberal ideology espoused enthusiastically by Margaret Thatcher and Ronald Reagan. Along with this, capitalism has been an article of faith since 1980. Large corporations lobby, fund political parties, and use their financial resources to influence those who are most likely to further their interests. With this goes belief in minimizing welfare benefits, theoretically to spur people to greater effort. Inevitably there are people who fail in the competition and this is accepted as collateral damage. The advocates of neoliberalism contend that neoliberalism is about respect for the freedom of the individual and that capitalism has indeed brought real progress. It ignores the lack of freedom of those imprisoned in poverty, unable to rise above their circumstances. The gross domestic product has become our god and the common good has disappeared from political discourse. Thus, although the origin of the pandemic lies elsewhere, neoliberalism and oppression have contributed to its severity by fueling poverty.

Poverty and oppression were the background from which liberation theology emerged in the 1960s in Latin America. Gustavo Gutiérrez wrote his *Theology of Liberation* in 1973 as a theological reflection on the lives of the poor.[18] He saw the poor as central to the earthly mission of Jesus Christ. Even a cursory reading of the Gospels will confirm this. Jon Sobrino sees the "Reign of God" as the central and ultimate purpose of the church.[19] That Reign is both now as well as in the future and implies the progressive reign of love in human affairs. Christian lives should center on commitment to others, not only to those in the church but also to those outside. He sees academic theology and the traditions of the church as secondary, turning traditional theology upside down. He maintains that God's love is universal and salvation is for the whole creation. The struggle for justice is part of salvation history; social injustice is incompatible with the Reign of God. He regards those members of the church who advocate non-involvement in politics as accepting injustice. He points out that those who preach about an exclusively transcendent Reign of God as something to be hoped for in the future are not a threat to the state and do not get murdered (as were Jesus, some of his apostles, and, more recently, Archbishop Oscar Romero in San Salvador). Liberation theology has a clear method: first, to see and understand the problems of the poor as the *poor* see their problems; and secondly to judge or analyze these in the light of the Bible as the *poor* interpret it. Thirdly, a course of action is then devised by and with the poor.[20]

18. See Gutiérrez, *Theology of Liberation*.
19. Sobrino, "Central Position," 195.
20. Boff, "Epistemology and Method," 7.

In 1985, as the effects of neoliberalism became apparent in the United Kingdom, the report "Faith in the City" described the poverty found in "urban priority areas."[21] The writers of the report saw liberation theology as a challenge to the church to reexamine its priorities and methods. But the Church of England, with its established status, hierarchical structure, and the importance it attaches to doctrine and academic theology, is ill-suited to the grassroots approach that is liberation theology, where the poor decide for themselves their priorities and mode of action.

Liberation theology addresses the oppressive policies, the widespread poverty, and associated loss of life in England and is therefore highly relevant in England and other rich countries with similar issues. BAME communities are describing their concerns and protesting against discrimination. Some organizations are responding. Others are calling for changes in the tax system, and food banks have increased their service. The poor are not yet being heard. Perhaps, like the Israelites being led out of Egypt, their spirit is broken (Exod 6:9). Arundhati Roy writes:

> Historically, pandemics have forced humans to break with the past and imagine their world anew. This one is no different. It is a portal, a gateway between one world and the next. We can choose to walk through it, dragging the carcasses of our prejudice and hatred, our avarice, our data banks and dead ideas, our dead rivers and smoky skies behind us. Or we can walk through lightly, with little luggage, ready to imagine another world. And ready to fight for it.[22]

The church needs to consider how it can better support the poor. As a society we need to consider what we worship. This is the choice before us.

---

21. Report of the Archbishop of Canterbury's Commission on Urban Priority Areas, *Faith in the City*, 63–65.

22. Roy, "Pandemic is a Portal," paras. 48–49.

19

Wondering in the Wilderness

Victoria L. Garvey

WE'VE SPENT ALMOST A whole liturgical year: the latter part of Lent 2020 and presumably going through Easter and maybe the Day of Pentecost 2021 in a kind of wilderness called COVID-19. In this country, there's been the added and seemingly eternal windstorm of an election off the wheels. And what does the life of faith—especially the life of faith recorded by our ancestors millennia ago—have to say to us in the twenty-first century?

The whole Bible, Genesis 1—Revelation 22, is a vast gathering of thoughts and remembrances and dreams and poetry and legal stuff, a potpourri of peoples' experiences with the Living God and with one another. One of the things the biblical writers did brilliantly was to remember reverently, and based on and emboldened by those memories, to push forward persistently. They used important experiences from their past to understand and interpret experiences in their present.

One of the great themes of the whole Bible is Journey; it shows up all over the place. Think Israel on the way from Pharaoh's Egypt to the promised land or Jonah's rocky ride to Nineveh or Jesus' carefully constructed way (in the synoptic Gospels, anyway) from Galilee to Jerusalem. And speaking of ways, there's that whole "way of the Lord" thing from Abraham's understanding that the way of the Lord was the journey marked by righteousness and justice (Gen 18:19) to the initial title for early Christians: People of the Way. Within that large theme of journey, a close relative motif is pocketed: it's called Wandering in the Wilderness.

Wilderness is one of those important words in the Bible, and because of its weightiness there, it gets a lot of play throughout Jewish-Christian traditioning, both in reality: wilderness is a real identifiable feature of the planet's geography, and first the People of Israel and then Jesus spent some quality time there; and after them the desert mothers and fathers and the Celtic Christians. And metaphorically: wilderness is a place humans have recognized in themselves, in the circumstances of their lives, from our biblical ancestors to ourselves.

In the Bible, the word wilderness, sometimes translated desert or abyss, appears in English (NRSV) some 449 times: in the Hebrew Bible, in the New Testament, and even in the lesser known books of the Apocrypha. It becomes a kind of controlling metaphor for the most formative times in the lives of our ancestors in the faith. That is, it's a time/place when they're untethered from everything they know and think they can count on as reality, and those sturdy ways of ordinary life vanish. It's when they learn who they are and what they're capable of doing and being.

Most people, if they think of it at all, remember the forty-year meanderings of the Israelites on their way to the promised land (Exodus—Deuteronomy). But this is just one of the large, more famous primal experiences. There are others, minor in the sense that they don't go on for four decades, but in their own ways as important: painful, informative, hope enfolding.

But before we get into the practicalities of those stories, a word about wilderness itself. Ever been to there? The deserts of the United States, for instance, or the Negev in southern Israel? Or other sorts of wilderness? There's a "terrible beauty" out there and also some real risk. No one—at least none of our biblical ancestors—goes into the wilderness unless they are compelled to do so in some way. The sun is so hot that it burns your skin by day. At night, when the sun goes down, it gets frigid. And the wind blows the sand into your face and it stings. And the wind erases your footsteps; it's hard to know whence you've come in the wilderness and it's hard to know where you're going. There's hardly any water in the wilderness so nothing much grows. You can starve in the wilderness with no food and you can die of thirst. Fear is the watchword out there. No one goes into the wilderness unless they are compelled to do so.

You can lose your sense of yourself in the wilderness. It puts you off balance. All the known boundaries with which you perimeter your life are gone. Sound familiar yet? You can lose yourself in the wilderness and you'll be afraid. But here's an odd little thing about the experience: Without all your familiar things around you, without your recognized assumptions of who you are and how the world works, you can also find yourself there. You can be found there. No one goes into the wilderness unless they are compelled to do so. And no one really emerges from the experience by themselves.

Back to the Bible and some of their wilderness periods. They are remembered by the various biblical authors as important in their history because of the things that were learned there, because of the hope that rose out of what seemed to be impossible situations, because they always emerged from the wilderness, stronger, more confident in themselves, more ready to face and move forward into an uncertain future.

You can look up the story of Hagar the Egyptian in Genesis (12–21, but especially 16 and 21) if you're curious. Hagar, whose name means "the stranger" or "the foreigner," and her little boy, Ishmael, whose name means "God will hear," or even "man of God," are both aptly named. They don't get much ink in our Bibles, appearing in only two stories and a footnote or so. So it might help to rehearse with you their backstory. God had come out of nowhere to call Abraham and Sarah to a new life, a new land, blessing, and children, something of a shock to people who'd been collecting the equivalent of Social Security for more than a decade. Chapters race by as do the years; and although they find a new land and blessing here and there, they're childless still at the ages of a hundred and of ninety or so, and apparently not for lack of trying.

It's then that Sarah determines to take matters into her own hands. God's either forgotten or changed the divine mind or something, so she suggests that Abraham take a substitute and there's this handy foreigner, a servant, who's available. Abraham doesn't hesitate and no sooner do they meet than Hagar becomes pregnant. This doesn't please Sarah nearly as much as she'd anticipated so she pitches the pregnant Hagar out into the wilderness where they all assume she'll die, wilderness being wilderness. Out she goes in fear of what awaits. But instead of slow death, she runs smack into, of all things and improbable as all get out—this is the wilderness after all—a spring of water. And more. God's out there too and gives her the first full annunciation speech in all of the Bible about the child growing in her womb even as she and God speak out in the middle of nowhere. In this place of fear and danger and death, she is promised life and a child of whom she and God will be inordinately proud.

Fast forward another ten or so years. Hagar's back with the family and the embryo has become a growing boy and Sarah's got one of her own as well; Isaac, finally born. All is well with the double family for a pitifully short interval until Sarah's confusion and overly protective hovering over her own child prompt her again to pack up that stranger and, this time, her son.

Although Hagar and the unborn Ishmael had dodged the wilderness bullet the first time out, as far as she and Ishmael and Abraham and Sarah are concerned, this second exile must surely lead to double death. Talk about fear of a nonexistent future. But there's God again with a well of water this time and more good news, a gospel in miniature actually, for her and her son who already lives up to his name as the one whom God hears. "Don't be afraid," says the God who's been faithful thus far; and she's not afraid. Frederick Buechner says of this little story that it tells us "how in the midst of the whole unseemly affair, God, half tipsy with compassion, went around making marvelous promises and loving everybody and creating great nations like the last of the big-time spenders handing out hundred-dollar bills."[1] The wilderness, symbol of despair and death and unquenchable grief, has become for this woman and her son a place of hope realized, of a future unimagined.

Fast forward to Exodus, to young Moses escaping Egypt with a price on his head. And where does he escape to? The wilderness, that place of death. And what does he find first? A well of water and a community, and eventually a God who calls him to a new life.[2] This little story, often ignored, is a kind of reversal of Hagar's, she an Egyptian slave of Israelites; he an Israelite slave of Egyptians. Both running to the wilderness for their lives. Both finding water in the desert and a new community, she with her son and eventually Egypt, he with a wife and eventually a son and then the infant community Israel and both encountering a God who calls them forward into a new life.

Arguably the most famous wilderness wandering story: Israel from Egypt to the promised land. The hike from slavery to settlement takes forty years and several books, Exodus, Leviticus, Numbers, Deuteronomy, and much of Joshua to tell. The Israelites didn't want to go; resisted Moses and his leadership; didn't want to follow the lead of some unknown God that

---

1. Buechner in the blog with fragments of his writings having to do with the readings of the day in Textweek.com for 2 Pentecost A, 2014.

2. Exod 2:15–22.

Moses had met in the middle of nowhere. Nobody goes into the wilderness willingly.

But there were those promises: return to the land once peopled by ancestors they'd forgotten they had, a freedom they'd never believed possible, a partnership with the God of all the earth. But once they left the land of oppression, instead of the milk and honey they were promised, they got wilderness and lostness and thirst and hunger and failure of confidence in their leader, their newfound God, and themselves. They got wilderness. Promises may have been spoken, but who can live by words alone? Hope has been proclaimed, but the horizon keeps disappearing in the endless shifting sand.

But the God who had appeared to Hagar in this wasteland was present still: in water where only rocks abound, in food where resources are nil, in healing where the pain seems all-consuming. And lest you think the point of this whole exercise is to help you understand that God is always with us—including in this season of COVID-19 and post-election madness—and God is, there's another thing our ancestors learned that's at least as important. Michael Walzer's *Exodus and Revolution* concentrates on the wilderness wandering of that period and ends with something like this: Everywhere we live is Egypt. All of us are on the way to a promised land. The only way to get there is through the wilderness. And to get through it, we have to go together. Community. One cooperating with another and another and another. That's how we get through.

One of the great things our ancestors remembered about this experience of the wilderness is that they had to rely on one another. It was in this period wandering around lost and confused that former slaves begin to form community, transform from no people at all to the People of God, to covenant partners with the living God.

Later, the prophet Hosea (especially chapters 1–3) picks up on this when he opines that the wilderness wanderings constituted the most important part of Israel's history. In that place with its difficult experiences, they had the luxury of being alone with God and with one another, able to form the kind of relationships that endure even the worst external circumstances.

And even later, an Isaiah, trying to pull his own contemporaries out of the gloom and chaos of the most catastrophic period of the Bible, a period when all of the tenets of Hebrew religion seemed to have been destroyed— land overtaken by others; last king of Israel taken into exile; the temple demolished; the divine promises to Abraham and Moses in tatters—Isaiah takes a page from the old family album, the sections on wilderness, and uses them to rally his people's hope: "Comfort, comfort, my people," he says, and reminds them of the mountains made low and the valleys lifted from the old Exodus—Deuteronomy stories (see Isa 40). Your ancestors made it, even if it did take forty years; we're going to make it too. And they did with the help of God and one another.

There are, in the Hebrew Bible, more stories of new beginnings hatched in what appear to be impossible circumstances, but we turn now to the Early Christian Scriptures with the most famous wilderness story found there: Jesus's testing. Matthew, Mark, and Luke tell the story, each in his own way, from Mark's sparse two verses (Mark 1:12–13) to Matthew's and Luke's more expansive tellings (Matt 4:1–11; Luke 4:1–13). In all three of these Gospels, the testing in the wilds takes place after Jesus' baptism and just before he begins his public ministry. It's a kind of test, and it takes how long? Of course, another forty—days this time, not years. The voice at his baptism had heaped praises on him: "my son, beloved . . . well pleased." The testing functions as a kind of final exam before he begins his teaching and preaching and healing. "Son of God?" There have been other folks called sons of God, some good, some not so hot: David was one, so were kings and prophets back in the earlier tradition. So, what kind of Son of God will this one be?

All three Gospels tell us that it was the Spirit who either led (Matthew and Luke) or drove (Mark) Jesus into the wilderness. Hagar and Moses had come upon a source of water—symbol of life—there. Hosea and Isaiah found the wilderness itself a source of life and hope, and countless other writers, too, had found to their astonishment, that the wilderness, place of desolation and death for millennia, had become for them, beyond all human reason, fecund territory, where community is born and grows, confidence is found, courage can be proven.

We know the story well: Jesus. Examiner. Three tests—in Matthew and Luke—all of which Jesus aces. His conversation partner out there is called devil or "Satan"; devil from the Greek *diabolos* meaning "one who throws things around" and *satan* from the Hebrew meaning "one who questions," "tests." And throw around beguiling possibilities it does. The tests are all about power: Of material power—the bread. Of political power—the kingdoms of the world. Of magical power—hurling off a rock with angel saviors. Jesus could feed himself and all the hungry people he met; he could be stronger than mighty Rome, so throw off oppression; he could wow the crowd with supernatural power and even manipulate God. It must have been downright tempting. Talk about jumpstarting your ministry.

But these are also questions of identity. What kind of a son of God . . . ? As we learn from the stories in the rest of the Gospels, Jesus was not an *abra-k'dabra* sort. He didn't want to wow folks with his divinely-inspired prowess. He wanted to enact the kingdom of God in his person in their midst so they'd know how they should act. That they too could act in godly ways.

The one who throws things all over the place was testing to see if Jesus is confused about what really matters, about who he is really called to be, and to see if he can be lured down paths that seem alluring at the moment but do not lead to the life he is called to live.

Jesus, despite artistic renderings of the wilderness tests, is not out there alone. He goes, still wet from his baptism with those words ringing in his ears: "son, beloved . . . well-pleased." He's loved, and that makes all the difference. And when he steps into his ministry a verse after the testing is done, he will not go alone. Yes, God is always with him, but taking a page from those who've braved the wilderness before him, he gathers around himself a growing community. And it's in community that he does the work he was sent to do, even to the end.

We've all known, even before I started nattering on about these biblical tidbits that I so love, that the answer of how to get through a wilderness is community. The Israelites knew it, even though it took forty years for them to get with the program. And Moses and Hagar. Naomi learned it from Ruth. The sibling rivals of Genesis, especially those twelve at the end of the book, finally learned it. And all those others who slogged through difficulties together in the Hebrew Bible. Jesus knew it even before he started being Jesus-y, taking care of all and sundry with a little help from his friends. And those tiny communities in Corinth and Rome and Thessalonica. And the Desert Fathers and Mothers and the Celts. Us too, mired in the sands of our own wildernesses of 2021.

Everywhere we live whether it's the United States or Africa, Europe or Asia, is an Egypt. We people of faith believe there's a kind of promised land over the horizon. But to get there, we have to slog through this wilderness of COVID—and election chaos—for a bit longer. What we've got is each other and the God who stands behind us all. And that is enough and more than enough.

20

I Believe . . .

Rosie Harper

It has been strangely moving to say the creed during lockdown. So much of what made us feel connected has been unplugged, and standing almost alone in the church building trying to create a sense of worship and preaching into thin air is a lonely business. In that context inviting people you cannot see to join with thousands, maybe millions of other people you cannot see in the words of the creed does feel like being logged into a spiritual World Wide Web.

Even those with whom you disagree on almost every point of ethics and theology will be saying the creed. As the church emerged, we, half intentionally and half by accident, made this contract about our identity and it has survived the test of time. No one Christian understands or believes it in exactly the same way, but nevertheless when we choose to say it we willingly place ourselves within the body of people who name their faith this way.

The pandemic raised all sorts of questions, especially about our worship, but we didn't have a punch up about the creed. It proved itself to be real and solid in a mighty virtual world. This is extraordinary, because the accelerated move online has thrown our grasp of reality and truth up in the air and we have yet to see where the pieces will land. Will we ever say again "I know" with any confidence?

The context is significant. Religion cannot but express itself within the spirit of the time. We have no other language and unless we are contextual, we cannot be incarnational. For example, no one under fifty grew up in a world where we assumed that reason was supreme.

We were basically still telling the story of God in Enlightenment terms and it seemed to work. The years after the Reformation were explosive times of growth and influence for the church. We grew in numbers and were given prominence, authority, and an influential voice in society. During those years, we tailored our story to fit in the new universe. Like it, our religion became solid, precise, and mechanical. Scouring the Scriptures, we came up with a clearly articulated, highly understandable religion. We determined all the right doctrines, systematized them in books.

We devised a proper doctrine for God, Jesus, human nature, sin, redemption, and the afterlife. We perfectly mirrored the culture. We became steeped in certitude, confident we had the right doctrines. The culture was looking for dependable answers to spiritual questions, and we had answers aplenty. Here are the roots of that confident phrase we still hear today: "The Bible clearly says."

Part of that worldview involved an extraordinary human self-confidence. A belief that whatever the universe threw at us we could fix. We were aware that there was stuff we didn't know, but that was temporary. We didn't know it yet. We couldn't fix it yet. But we would. It was important that there were answers out there and that we just had to find them. The evidence seemed to support this and we walked blindly into the misuse of the world's resources, the overuse of antibiotics, and many other potentially fatal errors because we calculated that we could think ourselves out of anything.

Quite naturally this became part of the way the church worked on its issues. That which at its very core is mysterious and ineffable was rationalized—almost into oblivion. On my bookshelves are various books that offer "proof" for the resurrection. If you really thought this through, they argue, you would see that it must have happened. It was access to the truth exclusively through a certain type of logic.

When challenging ethical matters came up they were approached in the same way. We can fix this. Think it through. Find the answer. There is a large elephant's graveyard of reports commissioned by the Church of England all trying to fix deep problems through reason. They were done in full confidence that there was a "right," a "true" answer. Our challenge was to find it. We super-spiritualized the endeavor, calling it a search for the mind of God.

The seeds for the disintegration of this way of negotiating life were planted at the beginning of the twentieth century, but the pandemic has blown it out of the water. All the parameters within which we lived have imploded. We no longer know what is real. We no longer know what is true. We feel disoriented in a world where time might no longer be linear and where multiple seemingly incompatible realities can coexist.

We had relied on our world functioning in solid, precise, or mechanical ways. Not at all! It wiggled around in ways that were random, chaotic, uncertain, and, mysterious. Neils Bohr first stirred the pot in the early 1900s. Atoms, he showed us, the tiny little units of matter that make up the universe, are not solid after all. The table, once the very picture of solidness, became decidedly not so. It is made up of empty space and electrical charges. Okay—a table appears to be solid when a cup is placed on it, but in the new universe, we all began to understand that the very concept of solidness is an illusion.

Then Einstein showed us that the universe isn't a precise place either. A ball thrown near the speed of light demonstrates that time and space are not as constant and absolute as we thought. The new universe became unsolid, illusory, relative, and no longer absolute. Heisenberg gave us a universe that is fundamentally unknowable. He showed us it is philosophically impossible to understand the basic nature of things. We can know where the little balls that make up the universe are, but not how fast they're going. Or, we can know how fast they're going, but not where they are. Fifty percent of reality is inaccessible to us at all times. The nature of things became, once again, unknowable.

In the early part of the last century, these physicists changed our universe. Solid gave way to unsolid. Certainty gave way to mystery, and absolute gave way to relative. Our universe became a vastly different place. For the last fifty years, our society has been hard at work rebuilding itself in response to quantum physics, just as it did in response to Newton several centuries ago.

This new world has upset the old order of politics. Fifty years ago, someone's political "ism" was precise, solid, and unquestionably "right." But as a fuzzier, less solid universe overtakes our imagination, we are hard at work rethinking how we do politics. It has thrown up the curveball of Trump, where somehow it didn't matter any more that what he said wasn't true. Or at least it wasn't the sort of truth we were used to. In global political dialog these days, many are working to integrate the truths of both democracy and socialism. It has become common to question if democracy is right for all nations at all times. These kinds of thoughts never occurred to us when the world was a solid place.

The concept of family has moved from fixed and certain to fluid and situational. Not long ago there was only one right way to do family. Even supposed fundamentals such as truth stopped being absolute. Fake news is just an expression of the loss of certainty.

Power is dispersed in seemingly random ways. Knowledge used to be power but today knowledge is accessible to everyone and power pops up in random and unexpected ways—for better or for worse.

So, what about the poor preacher, still standing firm on his Reformation-era absolute truths? In a world where few believe that any truth can be absolute, what is to become of solid, precise, absolute doctrines about God, Jesus, and the Bible? We were already in this place before March 23, 2020, but COVID-19 launched us into a whole new era. Overnight everything became virtual. We had to negotiate a world that might be populated by avatars—on Zoom we couldn't tell.

Nothing demonstrated this more than the lively conversation about the Eucharist. How, in a whole world of virtual reality, can you discern what is real and authentic? The leap of faith that we make when we take a piece of bread and call it the body of Christ already happened in a virtual way. We may have clothed mystery with physicality, but the whole expression of faith in the Eucharist demands the suspension of disbelief and the ability to see living faith in story. We are utterly dependent on the work of the Holy Spirit whether the priest says the prayer of consecration over the bread in front of the people or over the bread virtually in front of them and instead in front of someone's home computer. However, we have never done it like this before. This virus is bullying us into reexamining the interface between incarnation and virtual reality, and we feel ill-equipped to do it.

We won't be able to continue telling our story with the absolute certitude with which we've become so comfortable. That universe was changing anyway and now with the push from COVID it has gone away. It makes many Christians really uncomfortable . . . but we do have a Christian doctrine that can help us navigate this transition. It's the doctrine of the ineffability, or incomprehensibility, of God. It tells us that even when we felt confident and certain in our doctrines, we weren't. We never fully comprehended God anyway. All we ever had were temporary, incomplete, and inadequate thoughts about God and our God story. Once we reorient ourselves to the idea that God can never be contained in any thought we think, the rethinking this new era demands of us becomes somewhat less frightening.

As the unlocking begins, we all want to rebuild. Many hearts long for church to be again what it once was. Rebuild the old way because we liked it that way. We will have to see if we have the courage to admit that it wasn't that great any more. Rebuilding like for like will give us a pastiche of the church of a bygone era. There are many treasures we need to put into the ark to take with us. There will also be treasures we need to rediscover. Then start recreating something that is alive today.

When I was a young Christian in the sixties and seventies I was taught to ignore the heart. Faith was claimed to be objective, and, it turned out for many, therefore sterile. Numbers have plummeted because there has been almost no procreation. This generation is discovering that life and therefore faith *is* about the heart. It is about consciousness, mystery, empathy, purpose, creativity, love, God. We have also learnt as we staggered through 2020 that faith is about connectivity. Unless you are called to be a hermit, it is not a solo but a communal dance.

But our connectivity has changed. On Sunday morning at our church these days there is a Book of Common Prayer Communion Service that goes up online at 0800. Some people watch it then because that is their regular church time. Other people watch it at random times throughout the week. I actually prerecorded it on Saturday and scheduled it to go "live" in the morning. When was the "real" service? Does it matter? Who are the congregation? The people who already knew each other and faithfully log in at 0800? What about the people who watch in the week? Who are they? Are they still congregation even if they are not connected to one another except by what they experience? Do online congregations really exist?

The answer might be "no." In which case the depth of reimagining will have to be profound. If the church no longer has congregation as its embodiment then it's facing an existential crisis. Oxford Diocese for example is putting huge resources into starting 750 new congregations. So, when I say: "I believe" . . . and feel logged into a spiritual World Wide Web, I am afraid that I am logged into a memory. I hope it's more real than that, but post-pandemic I can't be sure.

21

Something Like Nothing Happens Anywhere

ALAN WILSON

IN 2020 SALES OF Albert Camus's 1947 novel, *The Plague*, boomed. It describes another pandemic's impact on the people of the French Algerian city of Oran. The mayor, a doctor, a priest, and others log the outbreak from their own particular perspectives. A disease that lay dormant in the city surfaces firstly among the rats then the human population. As it gathers pace, the citizens cannot imagine what effect it will have on them, and become fixated with figures. When the figures fall, they kid themselves that the plague has gone rather than gone underground.

The last word goes to Dr. Rieux. Unlike the citizens who think it is all over, he knows the plague "never dies or vanishes entirely." Jacqueline Rose, Professor of Humanities at Birkbeck, reviewed *The Plague* in the *London Review of Books*. She summarized its message thus: "The pestilence is at once blight and revelation. It brings the hidden truth of a corrupt world to the surface."[1]

The pestilence revealed the inequality of English life. Even as political leaders pushed a message of solidarity—"we're all in this equally together"—it was pretty obvious this was not generally the case. Death rates varied widely, closely mirroring deprivation indices. Lockdown in a detached property with a large garden, a loving partner, and a safe job that

1. Rose, "Pointing the Finger," para. 4.

could be tackled from home was a very different experience from that of most people. In general being low status did exacerbate hardship, but not universally. Rough sleepers were shoveled off the streets into disused hotels where they had safe shelter, food, a television, and a warm bed.

The church lockdown experience was very much more tolerable for well-organized parishes with new media know-how and squads of volunteers. They tended to be in more affluent areas. Lack of equipment and poor internet connectivity cut off great swaths of the population from churches, like schools. This did not only happen in rural areas. The pestilence revealed United Kingdom infrastructure to be patchy to say the least, including the healthcare system. People painted rainbows and clapped on their doorsteps for what is arguably, in sociological terms, the new national religion. It remains to be seen whether this affection can heal it and provide contingency for the future, after years of austerity, creeping privatization raking profits off the system (including the so-called "internal market"), and crippling debt arising from years of reckoning for the Private Finance Initiative.

Parishes' experience of lockdown depended greatly on how they related to their contexts as gathered and eclectic or societally engaged and dispersed communities. In 2019 I studied the suite of statistics known as "Statistics for Mission" for a large Evangelical benefice that serves a population of twenty-five thousand. On a whim, I wondered what the figures were for the same number of congregations serving the twenty-five thousand people who lived in more theologically diverse parishes next door—the same number of churches and ordained staff, the same population and in the same area of the country, though of course with great sociological granularity on a micro scale in both agglomerations.

Without getting lost in the detail, two very different patterns of engagement appeared from the comparison. The more Evangelical single benefice yielded much higher figures for youth and children's work, but a dramatically smaller number of "occasional offices" and a dramatically smaller fringe. Membership was actually lower than in the more diverse network of parishes next door. These actually had higher numbers of members, but exhibited a sawtooth shape around roll revision years, not evident in the larger benefice. Both datasets, however, showed declining numbers over ten years. Decline was slightly less marked in the more dispersed grouping, but followed an even trajectory. Meanwhile the more Evangelical neighbor showed a pattern shaped like an upside-down hockey stick, tailing off more rapidly in very recent years. In short, the dispersed and diverse parishes were in contact with a greater slice of the populations they served in a far greater variety of ways.

From a sociological point of view, the large single benefice specializes in Bonding capital. It has clear boundaries, and doctrine is the denominator of faith. People know whether they're in or out. The congregation coalesces around a basically unified body of beliefs and practices. It aims to attract newcomers by clearly focused teaching and discipleship, bringing them to conversion, and trying to make them feel good about being there when they join up. Often works, but there is a catch. It appears they can only gather so many people before a law of diminishing returns sets in and they hit a ceiling above which they cannot rise. At this point their evangelistic efforts seem to put off more people than they encourage and convert. The social impact for this benefice was around eight percent of population.

The other parishes are more diverse. They specialize in Bridging capital. They have low porous boundaries and large flabby fringes. They have many links to a range of individuals and organizations. Their catch is that attendance was very much more spasmodic and irregular. They relish occasional offices, and draw much energy from their fringe. Their good story is that they have many bridges into their community. So far so good but unless attention is paid to who crosses these bridges and why, and where they end up, they lose touch with the sources of energy upon which they must rely as voluntary organizations. Arguably they become so laid back they lose focus. Their impact figure among the populations they served, however, was around 25 percent, very similar to some figures for the taking up of online worship in the first lockdown.

Of course, all parishes build both Bridging and Bonding capital. What's interesting is the balance between them. The ideal church would be equally good at building both. Among clergy in COVID times, one sure diagnostic has emerged to define the balance of Bridging to Bonding capital. Some clergy, naturally attuned to building community beyond the congregation, reported being snowed under with funerals during the pandemic, sometimes more than one a day. Other clergy, Bonding capital specialists who tend to see non-members' occasional offices as an irrelevance to gospel ministry, report hardly any funerals.

COVID lockdown revealed some limitations of the attractional gathered model. You can't blow people's socks off with worship with the building closed and the worship group struggling on Zoom. Even if you succeeded, people who want such things already have God-TV and its ilk doing big cheerful worship on television. . . . The picture isn't uniformly poor. New people have joined online Alpha courses and the like, but generally many gathered congregations have found it very difficult to keep in touch with people.

This has been especially true sometimes with young people. Imagine a church with a hundred youth group members. Around ten come from strong church families. They have had quite a good pandemic, helping with online worship along with their families and generally enjoying being more at home in a more connected social milieu than either older church members or their secular friends. So far so good. Unfortunately, the other ninety less churched members have just gotten out of the habit and fallen off the network. The network will have to be rebuilt from the ground up after COVID.

Meanwhile more outwardly focused churches in villages and market towns have never worked as hard but have sometimes found new value and purpose. They had bigger fringes for a start and some communities have seen a central role for them at the heart of their response to the pandemic.

For at least the past two hundred years the great sign of how well a church was doing its job was the size of its congregation. When people encountered clergy at their parties they asked them "how large is your flock?" Evangelistic strategies were all about increasing the number of "bums on pews." Now, after a year in which there have been almost no bums on pews, the future value of this statistic is uncertain. What is certain is that with all churches and clergy exhausted, those with the most resource to rebuild will be those that have the broadest and strongest social networks. The great sign of a strong church will be the quality of its engagement with its context, not the quantity in church on Sunday morning, bums on pews.

A particular feature of the Church of England is its parish system. This places every person, every blade of grass it is said, in someone's parish. National service personnel were told "if it moves, salute it. If it doesn't, paint it." The parish system has had its own version of this approach. It has involved a duty to christen, marry, or bury all comers, along with various civic, charity, and social functions, most of which have very little to do with religion.

For years some people have been saying the parish system is a busted flush. When England was a Christian country, it made sense that, failing a few Nonconformist opt-outs, the Church of England was every citizen's birthright. As church and society moved apart, the future could only lie in gathered committed congregations. These would number a smaller proportion of the population, but gradually, community by community, enthusiastic believers would spread the word "like they did in the early church" and bring their neighbors back in to church. In the meanwhile what remained of the old order was set at a discount. The fringe didn't really matter because it was not lukewarm at best.

Now online activity has burgeoned. Any episcopal call to go online in 2019 would have been met with general disbelief or indifference. Then everybody had to do it in short order or there would be no Easter. Very often online is discussed in terms of its limitations and deficits. But there are benefits of size, reach, and interactivity on the new digital fringe. It encompasses a far greater variety of outlook as well.

And what of "growing the church?" If I ran a supermarket, I would of course work to delight my weekly shoppers. But if I wanted the customer base to grow seriously, I would focus on delighting people who only looked in occasionally for a tin of cat food. That is the group from which most of the firm's future growth would come, if only I can grow the network and their sense that my supermarket adds value to their lives. The last thing I would do is limit service to customers with a loyalty card.

So, one positive effect of lockdown religion might be to kill off a few obsolete and deeply unappreciated habits, whilst opening the door on a fuller, more varied, versatile, and people-centered response to the fringe. It would also serve shut-ins and other parishioners who have conventionally often received short shrift from their churches. To do this the church must maintain and develop its use of media it has habitually treated as a hobby for geeks rather than the stuff of significant pastoral relationships. The future, we are told, is local and distributed.

Suddenly the parish with its broad reach and low threshold looks less like a relic of the past. The new fringe is a place where Bridging and Bonding social capital can both grow, if only the churches' offerings are well earthed in locality, diverse rather than exclusive, and take people seriously on their own terms, not as pew fodder.

And what sort of clergy are most likely to flourish in this emerging kind of environment? Technological know-how, the historic qualification for vicars to dabble in online activity, is unnecessary. Most communities now contain plenty of that anyway. That does not have to be the vicar's job, and more people of a wider spectrum of generations may be engaged in the life of the church if it isn't.

The principal virtue required for hybrid online/physical networked vicars will not be religious or digital geekier yet. In 1962 the journalist Paul Ferris interviewed an old-fashioned Anglo-Catholic slum priest and observed: "He is happy. He likes people and people like him. He is *there* which is perhaps what matters." Clergy and congregations can now be there, not exclusively but radically inclusively.

22

Nevertheless

A Bridge from Despair to Hope

Robert D. Hughes

It is still cold and dark at night here in Chicagoland as I struggle with the Parkinson's Disease that makes my fingers wobbly and fat, trying to get the words down on the iPad to say what the remnant of my brain is thinking. Thinking about how to convey what it feels like to be coming out at the end of the long winter, the dark night of soul and Republic overshadowed by virus, isolation from loved ones in family and church, and frightened by how close it came to my dying generation leaving as its legacy a failed democratic republic devolved into a plutocracy flaunting its love for the original sins of the republic.

Hope. I try to remember what that is when the new shoots of spring are buried under another load of snow and my brain has less and less of its own dopamine with which to be glad. We live in a wonderful senior living accommodation, but we are so often losing good new friends who die or become ill beyond the ability of our place to cope. One of the joys of having the rules relaxed, so we can eat again in common, is seeing who is still alive. I am humbled by the ability of so many residents to bear far more pain than I have with much more patience. It's impossible to be an optimist here. Things are not going to get better for most of us any time soon in ways understood by the world. The Parkinson's Disease will see to that in my case. Yet we still have much for which to be grateful, and there does seem to be some room between despair and optimism, a space usually called hope. But what is hope, and where do we find it? Each of us must come to our own answers, but one of mine comes, oddly enough, from thinking about the fourteenth century, and the great Christian mystics of that era, especially Strasbourg Dominican preacher John Tauler and English Anchoress Julian of Norwich.

I first began to understand the devastation that was fourteenth-century Europe in a class taught by Professor Harry A. Miskimin, and his presentation of his own work on fourteenth-century France as seen in population statistics alongside evidence from money and banking. The facts point to real calamity: villages in France were depopulated by as much as 2/3 to 3/4, and the economic collapse was so bad that economic measures of money and banking did not return to thirteenth-century levels until the eighteenth.

What were the causes of this disaster? Taking from both Miskimin and Barbara Tuchmann's brilliant *A Distant Mirror*, as well as Bernard Mc-Ginn's *The Harvest of Christian Mysticism in Medieval Germany*, we get a list something like this:

1. An implacable Foe. The forces of Islam, mostly Turks and Arabs, were beating Christians on every front.

2. A global pandemic as wave after wave of plague took an unimaginable death toll, with no understanding of the nature of the disease or of its transmission by fleas on the rats stowing away on all the ships plying the Mediterranean.

3. Despite those devastating two, the European nobility and royalty were willing to pay extravagant prices for silks and spices that could only be had from Arab traders through port city states such as Venice and Genoa. Since the Europeans had little of their own goods to trade, there was an enormous balance of trade problem with most of the gold ending up with the Arab traders.

4. That produces the first real voodoo economics: solve the very real bullion crisis by debasing the currency. That did not turn out well. Sort of like helping poor folks by giving the ultra-rich a tax cut.

5. The divided papacy (Rome and Avignon, France) marked the end of the *Pax Ecclesiae*, as the feudal order collapsed. The result was the

Hundred Years' War between France and England in which all the emerging European powers took part. If you were a peasant, or even the citizen of one of the new cities, the main question every day was whose army would be in town this week, raping and pillaging, taking all your food in exchange for a new wave of plague. The old feudal system did not yield gently to the rise of modern nation states, and in the interim, life was indeed nasty, brutish, and short. And speaking of food, there was an occasional famine.

6. The predominant theologies and philosophies of the time we group under the title Nominalism are important developments in the birth of modernism. But their rigorous skepticism, though it suited the mood of the time, brought cold comfort for its miseries.

Tuchman saw similarities to the horrors of the twentieth century, but the mix of implacable foe or rival, pandemic out of control, political differences so deep as to inspire violence, voodoo economics that make the poor poorer, endless war, the weakening of trusted institutions, all sound only too familiar early in the twenty-first.

Of course, there were small sparks of light as well. Library Science advanced by alphabetizing authors' names, replacing a system of Platonic Ideas. English Franciscan William of Ockham added his famous "Razor" to the foundations of modern scientific method laid by another English Franciscan, Roger Bacon. Art continued to evolve, one channel leading to the grotesque as seen in Grunewald's paintings of the crucifixion. The evolution of civil life continued to move from feudal to mercantile. The severe depopulation meant fewer workers; pay increased substantially, raising many to the ranks of the growing bourgeoisie.

Of great solace to me, however, was the abundant outpouring or harvest of Christian mysticism. First the Rhineland mystics, all followers of Meister Eckhart who seemed not to be snared by the charges of heresy against the Meister. Bernard McGinn is the source of the best scholarship on this topic. The main characters in this period after Meister are Henry Suso, Johannes Tauler, Ian van Ruysbroec, Margarita Ebner, and the unknown author of the *Theologia Germanica*. Each taught there were depths of one's relationship to God that lay beyond what the church and its ministers offered, though not necessarily without them. This rebirth of the word in the ground of the soul, in a third begetting of the word, or a second incarnation of the word, had been pretty metaphysical in Eckhart. In his followers it became an experiential and pastoral relationship so close it could only be characterized as friendship. Indeed several or all of them were linked in a society called Friends of God, which the church authorities often assigned to the dumpster labeled Brethren of the Free Spirit. Tauler's preaching of a direct personal relationship to God through Christ, available to ordinary Christians, also became standard fare for the Lollards and John Wycliffe who was active in this period. Indeed Tauler became very popular among Protestants. He was especially influential on Luther and the Pietists as well as Wesley's Methodism and the Pentecostalism that grew out of it. I too think Tauler is a bit bemused about how wide his influence has been.

Meanwhile, the narrow channel did not protect England from the ravages of the century. They were one of the two major combatants in the Hundred Years' War. The English had so much fun with it that they internalized it as their own War of the Roses, which ended in the bourgeois reign of the Tudors. England had its fair share of plague, and was home to as many precursors of the Reformation as Germany.

It also had its own clutch of mystics. There is not, to my knowledge, any direct link with their German spiritual kin, and they bear only a family resemblance to each other, except for a preference for Middle English over Latin and a spirituality as good for ordinary folks as for nobles. Among them notables include whoever wrote the *Ancrene Riwle*, Richard Rolle of Hampole, the one known only as the author of the *Cloud of Unknowing*, Margery Kempe, and the Rose of English mystics, Dame Julian of Norwich.

Julian was the first woman to publish a book in Middle English, and what a book it turned out to be! It comes in two forms, the short text and the long text. They tell the same basic story of a woman in her thirties who became an anchoress by having herself walled into a small room attached to St Julian's Church in Norwich. Actually, it had two small windows, one facing outside and one facing into the church. People could come to her to talk. Small gifts and food and fuel were passed in, and waste of all sorts was passed out. Through the interior window she could also participate in services and receive sacraments. This practice was not uncommon at the time.

Anyway, that's about all we know, not even if her real name was Julian or taken from the name of the church. In her thirties she fell ill and asked that the illness be to the point of death so that her compassion might be increased. She received the last rites but survived. During her recovery she reports receiving thirteen showings or revelations from God about her theological questions and anxieties. Her revelations cover most doctrines of the faith in a charming, delightful manner that is also orthodox and groundbreaking at once, and shows signs of a superior education for the time, including good Latin and some Augustine as well. The book was and has remained immensely popular with the devout and academic alike. The latter have abundant interpretations of nearly every possible matter. It really is remarkable that a woman born in the mid-fourteenth century who lived well into the fifteenth should be a growth industry in the twentieth/twenty-first.

Two of Julian's teachings are particularly original and still relevant. The first, shared with Anselm some centuries earlier, is of the motherhood of God, specifically for Julian that Christ is our Mother. This produces some arresting gender-bending grammar, but also some delightful theological moves, such as a meditation on the wound in Christ's side out of which he both births and nourishes us, at once vagina and breast, opened and flowing at the time of his saving death. There are also some very challenging reflections on the implications of Christ as our Mother for the Trinity.

Julian's second remarkable teaching is her great outburst by Jesus that "All shall be well, and all shall be well, and all manner of thing shall be well." Some have accused her of falling into empty optimism here, but this ignores the context. This assertion of a "sure and certain hope" is surrounded on all sides by stark and serious contemplation of sin and its consequences for human creatures and for God. Indeed, Julian embodies for us the difference between optimism—the belief that things are automatically getting better, in denial of evidence to the contrary, and hope—the belief that all shall be well in spite of evidence to the contrary, because God rejoices to be our Father and rejoices also to be our Mother. What Jesus actually says to Julian, after graphic descriptions of sin, is "sin is unavoidable; nevertheless all shall be well."[1]

Furthermore, the two teachings are related. It is Christ as our Mother who reassures us that all shall be well, who also shall make all things well. I am reminded of that great moment in Peter Berger's *A Rumor of Angels* when he contemplates the instinct of a parent confronting a catastrophe with a child to say something like "It's going to be alright. We are going to get through this. You will be ok." As Berger says, that's either a damned lie or a theological affirmation. It is precisely the latter for Julian, for it is Christ our mother who reassures us that Nevertheless All Shall be Well, who can

---

1. My translation from the Middle English "behovely," which is usually translated necessary but can also mean unavoidable or inevitable.

and will make all manner of thing to be well. Even from this distance the sermons of Tauler and the Revelations of Julian glow like reigniting sparks from the dark disaster that was the fourteenth century, grounding a sure and certain hope in the nature of God as friend and of Christ our Mother. Can we still share that hope?

For myself, sitting in the dusk towards the end of this life for me and for many I love, and a year lost to the darkness of isolation caused by the COVID-19 pandemic (to say nothing about all who have already died and will yet die from it), it helps to remember the horrors of the fourteenth century and the coals like Tauler and Julian already glowing with the wind of the Spirit building towards the coming purifying conflagration of the Reformation. Reading or rereading them in the dark nights of our collective soul may give us hope there are more options than lighting a candle of one's own or cursing the dark. May we not also sit in our darkness until our eyes adjust enough to see the sparks God already has glowing and ready to burst into flame? Black Lives Matter? Greta Thunberg and the environmentalism of our young? Bishop Michel Curry and the Jesus Movement growing into the Beloved Community? Or even all those sincerely seeking that more perfect Union promised by our Constitution? May we yet find those coals God is already raising up to lighten our darkness, and offer to be allies or even friends? The least we can do is cheer from the sidelines, "Burn baby, burn." For our God is a consuming fire, the living flame of love, who tells us "I know it's pretty bad and really hurts and the inevitability of sin is a terrifying mystery; *nevertheless*, all shall be well, dear friend."

Afterword

Good Grief

The Gains That Come Through Loss

MARTYN PERCY

As I REMARKED TO a close colleague the other day, grief is exhausting. His mother had just died in a care home. It was not unexpected, and in some ways, a mercy. But bereavement or loss have "form," and like a virus, live inside our heads and hearts, and freely stroll around the highways and by-ways of our conscious and subconscious. There is no vaccine for grief.

Rather like Judith Kerr's *The Tiger That Came to Tea*, grief involves entertaining an intrusive guest that settles down for a lengthy stay. It helps itself to our time and energy, distracts us when we are trying to concentrate on more important things, and stops us finishing even the most basic tasks. It tends to be untidy. It messes us up on the inside. Tasks that once took us no time at all now take forever. Energy levels drop. We are always tired; yet we cannot properly sleep.

Grief is normal. It is one price we pay for love. It is part of what it is to be a person—because we cannot be a person unless we are in communion with others, so we are always bonded. Even when alone, in our own heads, so to speak, we are connected. When bereaved, then, the mind plays around with a whole range of "What if . . . ?" and "If only . . . " scenarios. "What if I had spent more time with her?" "If only I had more time with him." Even seasoned practitioners of mindfulness will struggle to rein in the range of loves, losses, regrets, wistful hopes, and memories when grief goes viral. And then there is a long list of things that actually need to be done. The death to register. A funeral to plan. People to notify.

One of the most striking aspects of this pandemic has been the enormous and shared levels of exhaustion we experience. For some, the causes are obvious. Working for the National Health Service, as keyworker, or in any kind of frontline care and services, has never been more demanding. Teachers and lecturers have had to pull out all the stops to put resources online. Those caught in an endless cycle of Zoom meetings, or on Microsoft Teams, Skype, or other platforms that connect us, are discovering that these are far more demanding than meeting in the flesh.

Parents who have never taught in schools (frankly, that is most of us) have suddenly discovered just how much energy it takes to occupy their children with meaningful learning. Others are wearied by economic uncertainty, trying to manage their panic. Or exhausted by hostile and abusive home situations. Our space for socialization has been shut down by this pandemic. And our space for rationalization is dominated by maths: flattening the curve; keeping two meters apart; maintaining social distance. When everything becomes enumerated and measured in figures, we wince. We all have names; we are not numbers. But somehow, the COVID-19 crisis has subjected our existence to some pretty ruthless number-crunching.

But there is another hidden curve at work in society at the moment, and it is one that will be with us for much longer than this pandemic endures. Whilst we work hard to flatten one curve, this other, veiled viral phenomenon, is actually a *natural* feature of human existence: grief. Elisabeth Kübler-Ross (1926–2004) was a Swiss-American psychiatrist who researched near-death studies, but is probably best known for her bestselling book, *On Death and Dying* (1969). Kübler-Ross observed that grief typically went through a trajectory that had a kind of "curve." She outlined her theory as "the five stages of grief."

The first stage was shock or denial at the tragic news or loss: "I can't believe it" or "this can't be happening to me" would be typical reactions. Denial is a temporary psychological defense mechanism that gives us time to absorb news of change. It entertains a slim hope: if we continue to deny reality, or at least challenge it, this all might go away. The news we just heard could all be "a big mistake."

The second stage was anger, with those bereaved typically wailing "why me . . . it's just not fair." Anger allows us to blame someone or something else for this happening to us. Public inquiries after tragedies are frequently exercises in anger management and social catharsis. Individuals, senior management, the economy, health and safety, a hospital—all can be blamed for negligence.

Kübler-Ross' third stage was bargaining. This is the inner conversation we have in the foothills of bereavement. "I'll give my all to be at my daughter's wedding or son's graduation. I need more time." This is the natural reaction of those who are dying—an attempt to postpone the inevitable. We bargain to shelve the change. If there is more time, maybe—just maybe—we can find a way out of this.

Depression was Kübler-Ross' fourth stage. With the first three stages passed, the reality of change sets in. It is at this point we start to become aware of losses and with the changes we face. This has the potential to push us into a gloomy state—depressed and demotivated. Ennui kicks in when we reach a point of uncertainty about our future. "What's the point of trying?" is a typical sentiment.

The fifth stage was acceptance. The curve is downwards now, and towards flattening. As we realize that fighting the change was not going to make it go away, we move into stages of acceptance. This is not always a contented space, but it can be one of cheerful resilience. It can be stoic (a kind of weary resignation in the face of what must be), but is not necessarily joyous.

Acceptance is the end of the curve, and you might assume that at that point, you are on the home straight. Acceptance can indeed be a creative space that presses us to explore afresh and look for new possibilities. Indeed, this may be why the Kübler-Ross Five-Stage Model has been extensively used by management consultants and workplace psychologists to explain how organizations cope with failure or trauma.

Simply stated, consultants have adapted these stages in order to explain other kinds of "Change Curves." So when companies or institutions go through any major restructuring or redundancies, or for that matter governments and societies suffer a significant failure in their delivery of health or social care, the curve only flattens when a majority of people affected begin to arrive at consensus and acceptance. Until then, there is *unrest*. Like grief, this time is tiring, and utterly unsettled.

We are still in this "Curve of *Un*-rest." Ours is civil, personal, emotional, and social. Our collective and individual exhaustion is symptomatic of the emotion and energy expended, as we try to comprehend and cope with the changes taking place all around us, and face up to the trauma of all that is being lost. We shift uneasily between Kübler-Ross's first four stages for the time being, in a cyclical motion we can barely manage, let alone control. In grief, people will often report one day merges into another; they lose all sense of time. No wonder we are all so exhausted.

So is there anything to look forward to beyond weariness and stoic acceptance, and a yearning for the Old Normal? Apart, that is, from regaining some work-life balance, and a proper night of rest after a full day of work? Or perhaps a weekend that actually feels like it once used to? I have a couple observations.

First, we mostly associate viruses with terms such as "disease," "infection," "suffering," or "life-threatening." We immediately think of HIV, Ebola, Zika, or old-fashioned influenza. However, not all viruses are bad. As many virologists will testify, some viruses are good. They kill harmful bacteria, for example, whilst others live peaceably in the human body and exist to fight against more dangerous viruses. Just like protective bacteria (i.e., probiotics) that live inside us, we also have several protective viruses within our bodies (e.g., phages). Not all viruses are detrimental to human health. Some viruses have beneficial properties for our bodies, and they work within us, forming a symbiotic relationship.

Second, David Kessler—also an expert on grief and collaborator with Elisabeth Kübler-Ross—suggested that there might be something *good* to emerge from our grief. Kessler proposed a sixth stage: meaning. Now, finding meaning is not about shoehorning a crisis into a moral or spiritual interpretative straitjacket. That would demean the very real suffering and loss of so many, which for everyone is profoundly personal. Sometimes the search for meaning can be glib: a classic means of evading cold reality and some blunt home-truths.

Our reality is stark. So much has stopped—work, sport, enterprise, travel, and entertainment—we find ourselves living in a kind of universal Lent. To emphasize this moment, public religious life ceased too. This enforced "perpetual pause" has brought a halt to our frenetic pace of life and our breathless race to squeeze more and more out of each minute of every day. Indeed, the virus has replaced that breathlessness with another kind of gasping. Plans and projects are all on hold.

So, might there be some signs of *good* meaning emerging from this crisis? Perhaps. Adjusting to a different pace, and finding some deep stillness can regenerate our core sense of purpose. A core no longer geared towards frenetic busyness, or self-fulfilment, can become more fulsome and self-aware. This can make us more mindful of others—especially those who continually live in perpetual states of exile or with all manner of serious social restrictions. We only understand the gift of our freedoms when we experience their loss. The simpler way of life that is currently forced upon us may actually help us become more discerning—refounding our purpose, communities, and society on the essentials rather than the merely expedient.

This is all about perspective; learning to see the difficulties of the here and now as potentially part and parcel of a much bigger canvas. At times of concern and worry, some sage counsel by a much-loved Jewish preacher-cum-teacher is suggestive:

> Look at the birds of the air; they neither sow nor reap nor gather into barns, and yet your heavenly Father feeds them. Are you not of more value than they? And can any of you by worrying add a single hour to your span of life, or a single cubit to your height? And why do you worry about clothing? Consider the lilies of the field, how they grow; they neither toil nor spin, yet I tell you, even Solomon in all his glory was not clothed like one of these. But if God so clothes the grass of the field, which is alive today and tomorrow is thrown into the oven, will he not much more clothe you—you of little faith?[1]

Jesus's exhortation to avoid worrying would have seemed as curious to his original audience as it might to us now. After all, a Galilean rabbi suggesting that a region dominated by an occupying army, where freedoms were restricted, and life and death hinged on fickle decisions made by unaccountable authorities, must have seemed like blind optimism to most. They had plagues too. Yet the Gospels record Jesus saying "do not worry" or "do not be afraid" over seventy times. Yes, seventy. He says it a lot. Don't be afraid of the storm, or of sinking. Don't worry about lack of food or clothes. Don't worry about death. *"Do not be afraid . . . I am with you."*

So what of faith and fear in a time like this? Our English word "worry" was originally derived from the word *wyrgan*, meaning to "strangle," and of Germanic origin. In Middle English the verb gave rise to the meaning

---

1. Matt 6:26–30.

"seize by the throat and tear," and later to our word "harass," meaning "to cause anxiety." It is ironic that one aspect of coronavirus is that it takes the breath away. It is, literally, a "worrying virus."

Jesus' summons is simple: consider the world around you; become attuned to the cycles of life in all their depletion and abundance. We are being bidden towards a more contemplative perspective. This is not a call to adopt some kind of supine passivity. It is just that there is little point in worrying about things we can't control. The birds of the air and lilies of the field are instructive.

Unwelcome as this may sound, grief can be good. It prunes and pares us back to our core. That is why so many who experience bereavement will testify to feeling "raw" in the early stages. Rawness and exposure are not states we readily seek. But grief normally strips away the peripheral to make way for the essential. In fact, grief prepares us for growth. So, just as death is an inevitable part of all our lives, we should prepare for it. For our own, as well as those who are our nearest and dearest.

Remember that death is just nature's way of slowing us down. It stops us in our tracks, whether we are the bereaved—or the deceased. Like some of the good viruses that live within the human body, there is a goodness in grief. It helps us cope with trauma. Processing our loss percolates through our personhood, and what begins as an experience of exposure will often mature into one of enrichment.

Processing grief also changes our personal and social landscapes. Lives are now cherished more than livelihoods. Care becomes more essential than cash. We relearn to live as generously as we hope to receive. Compassion and empathy become our daily bread, and we learn to share this with others who are hungry for it. Prayer moves from frantic pleading to perspectives more contemplative. Faith, hope, and love can cast out fear. The realization of our mortality slowly sinks in, soaking our souls. Yet this does not sink us. As Harriet Beecher Stowe said, "the bitterest tears shed over graves are for words unsaid and deeds left undone." Grief *re-minds* us to pay attention, here and now, to who and what matters: do not prevaricate.

There was an advertising poster for the National Health Service some years ago that sought to recruit new nurses. The advert pictured a nurse cradling a newborn baby, and the caption read: "the first few minutes of life can be critical." Someone, however, had daubed some graffiti underneath, adding: " . . . and the last few can be a bit dicey too." Quite. This is a tender, liminal moment in our nation and communities. But cradling, holding, and caring for others at the beginning and end of life—and for all that bit we call "the middle" (the bulk of our lives)—is where our attention must return to.

As we progress through our Curve of Grief, our challenge is to progress beyond mere stoicism, and discover worthier ways to work and live. As a nation, I hope and pray we will get past our shock, anger, and denial. I hope and pray we will get past our instinct for blaming and retribution. I hope and pray we shall not just ask "what went wrong, then?" but take courage and ask "how then, shall we live?"

In this, I harbor some hope for our future. As Charles Schulz's Lucy might once have said to Charlie Brown, "Good grief is better than bad grief." Can we permit our grief to become the foundation of new, good, and generative futures? I believe so. It is in fully facing the ordeal of loss that we have the hope of realizing life-giving gain.

Contributors

Ellen Clark-King is the Dean of King's College London. She was ordained priest in the Church of England in 1994 and has served in Hereford; Cambridge; Newcastle upon Tyne; Christ Church Cathedral, Vancouver; and as Vice Dean and Canon for Social Justice at Grace Cathedral, San Francisco. Ellen is the author of two books: *Theology by Heart: Women, the Church and God* (2004) and *The Path to Your Door: Approaches to Christian Spirituality* (2011). She is currently exploring a Christian spirituality of leadership.

Sarah Cotes studied medicine in South Africa where she spent twelve years as a young person. Having worked her way up the career ladder in the United Kingdom she became a consultant in respiratory medicine and was committed to the National Health Service throughout her career. She is proud of having developed and led the respiratory service and undergraduate medical education in the hospital in Durham. She was also a magistrate, working in the adult and youth courts, and spent some years on the Independent Monitoring Board of a large prison in Durham. This broad experience made her very conscious of socioeconomic inequalities in the United Kingdom, especially insofar as they affect health and welfare. Following retirement and the death of her husband, she decided to take a new direction and pursue a lifelong but amateurish interest in theology and embarked upon the graduate diploma course in theology and religious studies that Durham University offers. She describes herself as the granny of the class and has greatly enjoyed the experience. Her South African background aroused her interest in liberation theology and her essay is the result of the confluence of this and medicine.

Jim Forest is the author of many books—see www.jimandnancyforest.com/books/, including *Writing Straight with Crooked Lines: A Memoir* (2020) *and Eyes of Compassion: Learning from Thich Nhat Hanh* (2021). During the Vietnam War he spent more than a year in prison for burning draft records. For twelve years he was General Secretary of the International Fellowship of Reconciliation, work that brought him to the Netherlands, where he still lives.

Gulnar (Guli) Francis-Dehqani was born and raised in Iran before moving to England in 1980, aged thirteen, following the events of the Islamic Revolution. She graduated from Nottingham University with a degree in Music before working for the BBC for several years, first at World Service Radio and later in the religious department of domestic radio. As well as having time off to raise three children, Guli has worked as a parish priest, educational chaplain, and diocesan curate training officer, becoming Bishop of Loughborough in 2017. She has written and spoken on a variety of subjects including in the areas of religious feminism and interfaith studies. Guli was appointed Bishop of Chelmsford in 2021. She serves as the Church of England's Bishop for Housing and is vice-president of the Conference of European Churches.

An educator for most of her life—a perspicacious first-grade teacher had her coaching others when she was six—**Victoria Garvey** has a passion for learning and teaching, and unsurprisingly, for the church. In her professional career she has taught at nearly every level from second graders through graduate school, but she has spent most of that teaching time at an Episcopal seminary (Seabury-Western in Evanston, IL) where she taught biblical languages and biblical theology, her doctoral area. Most recently, those passions for learning/teaching/church were fed in her position as Bishop's Associate for Lifelong Christian Formation in the Episcopal Diocese of Chicago where she even got paid for doing what she loves. These days, she serves on two faculties for the wider church, does occasional stints as speaker and preacher in congregations, and continues to speak locally, nationally, and occasionally, internationally, facilitates workshops, leads retreats, and writes now and again for national journals.

Robin Gibbons is a Patriarchal Priest of the Greek Catholic Melkite (Byzantine Rite) Church, ministering in England, and an Ecumenical Canon at Christ Church Cathedral, Oxford. He has worked in academic life for over thirty-five years in London, Twickenham, and Oxford. A liturgist, he also researches and writes on Eastern Christianity, spirituality, ecumenism, monasticism, and art. He is a Benedictine affiliate of Christ the Saviour Monastery, Turvey. He keeps cats, bees, writes poetry, and loves the environment.

Rogers Govender, MBE, is a South African priest ordained in 1985 at the Cathedral of the Holy Nativity in Pietermaritzburg, KwaZulu-Natal. Rogers is of South Indian descent, his forefathers and mothers having been indentured laborers who were part of the wave of migrants brought by the British colonial government to work in the sugar cane fields in Durban in the 1860s. In 2000 he moved with his family to Manchester, England, to be a parish priest. He was appointed Dean of Manchester in 2006. He is a student of liberation and contextual theology, and campaigns against racism and exclusion in church and society. Some of his interests include church growth, interfaith collaboration, climate change issues, and challenging hate crime.

Rosie Harper was born in London, and grew up in Norwich. She is both British and Swiss. After her first degree in music and English at Birmingham University she did post-graduate studies at the Royal Academy of Music, winning various prizes and awards including the prestigious Wagner Prize. She worked for many years as a professional singer, both in the United Kingdom and in Europe. Rosie now serves as the vicar of Great Missenden and Chaplain to the Bishop of Buckingham. Until recently she was chair of the Oxford Nandyal Education Foundation, a charity focused on capacity building in rural Indian schools. A member of General Synod, Rosie writes for the *Guardian*, was a panel member for Any Questions, and speaks around the country in debates on public philosophy. She is deeply committed to working for issues of justice and equality within and beyond the church. She is an active campaigner for LGBTI rights and also a patron of dignity in dying.

Robert D. Hughes, III, was the Norma and Olan Mills Professor of Divinity and Professor of Systematic Theology in the School of Theology of The University of the South, Sewanee, Tennessee. He taught at Sewanee from 1977 until his retirement in 2016. His book *Beloved Dust: Tides of the Spirit in the Christian Life* (2008) received the des Places-Libermann Award in Pneumatology from Duquesne University in 2010. He also wrote "The Holy Spirit in Christian Spirituality" for The Blackwell Companion to

Christian Spirituality (2005). He is a married Episcopal priest/theologian who is currently Theologian in Residence (Retired) at Grace Episcopal Church, Oak Park, IL.

Thomas Hughson, SJ, is emeritus on the faculty of Theology at Marquette University, Milwaukee, WI, USA. He served as Director and Superior of the Pontifical Biblical Institute-Jerusalem (1986–89) and was Director of Graduate Studies in the Marquette Theology Department for some years. His specialties are systematic theology (Trinity, Christology, pneumatology, ecclesiology) in cultural context, ecumenism, and most recently dialogue with archaeology on prehistoric religion. His publications include *Connecting Jesus to Social Justice: Classical Christology and Public Theology* (2013) and *The Holy Spirit and Ecumenism* (ed., 2016). "Neandertal Symbols: Neandertal Spirituality?," presented at an archaeological conference at the University of Turin, appears in the proceedings, NeanderAt2018 (2020). An invited book, *Neanderthal Religion: A Theologian Begins Dialogue with Archaeology*, is underway. His main pastoral activity has been spiritual accompaniment in light of the *Spiritual Exercises* of Saint Ignatius.

Alan Jones is Dean Emeritus at Grace Cathedral, San Francisco. He was awarded an OBE and is an honorary Canon of the Cathedral of Our Lady, Chartres. He was the Stephen F. Bayne Professor of Ascetical Theology at General Theological Seminary. He was also the Director and Founder of the Center for Christian Spirituality at General Seminary. His publications include *The Soul's Journey: Exploring the Three Passages of Spiritual Life with Dante as a Guide* (1995); *Passion for Pilgrimage: Notes for the Journey Home* (1999); and *Living the Truth* (2000).

Daniel Joslyn-Siemiatkoski is the Duncalf-Villavaso Professor of Church History at Seminary of the Southwest in Austin, TX, and its Dean of Community Life. He works in the fields of comparative theology, Jewish-Christian relations, and Anglican studies. He is most recently the author of *The More Torah, The More Life: A Christian Commentary on Mishnah Avot* (2018). As a priest he serves at both Southwest and St. David's Episcopal Church in Austin.

Shemil Mathew was born and brought up in Kerala, India, in a Christian family in the tradition of St Thomas. He first studied for a bachelor's and master's degree in English language and literature before achieving both bachelor's and master's degrees in theology from the University of Gloucestershire. Shemil has wide experience of working with Anglican Communion churches in Asia and Africa and has worked as a teacher in Sri Lanka. He was ordained in Peterborough Diocese after training at Cuddesdon where he also gained an MTh. While at Cuddesdon he cofounded AMEN (Anglican Minority Ethnic Network), an independent network to encourage vocations from minority ethnic communities. Shemil is currently the Anglican chaplain at Oxford Brookes University. He teaches contextual theology at Ripon College Cuddeson and for the Church Mission Society pioneer course.

A moral theologian in the Anglican tradition, **Lucinda Allen Mosher** is Faculty Associate in Chaplaincy and Interreligious Studies at Hartford Seminary, where she is Co-Director of the Master of Arts in Chaplaincy Program, Senior Scholar for Executive and Professional Education, and an affiliate of the Macdonald Center for the Study of Islam and Christian-Muslim Relations. Concurrently, she is Senior Editor of the *Journal of Interreligious Studies*, Rapporteur of the *Building Bridges Seminar* (an international dialogue of Christian and Muslim scholars), and Fellow Emerita of the Center for Anglican Communion Studies at Virginia Theological Seminary. She is the author of seven books, including *Toward Our Mutual Flourishing: The Episcopal Church, Interreligious Relations, and Theologies of Religious Manyness* (2012); she is the editor of eleven more, including (with Vineet Chander) the award-winning *Hindu Approaches to Spiritual Care: Chaplaincy in Theory and Practice* (2020) and the *Georgetown Companion to Interreligious Studies* (forthcoming 2022). Additionally, she has made numerous contributions to edited volumes and journals. An accomplished performer on several instruments, she is also the Music Director at St Mary's Episcopal Church, Green Cove Springs, Florida. Occasionally, she publishes on comparative theology and the arts.

Emma Percy is Chaplain of Trinity College Oxford and Chair of WATCH (women and the church). She is one of the first generation of women ordained priest in the Church of England in 1994. She is a feminist practical theologian and has long been an advocate for an inclusive church. She is the author of *Mothering as a Metaphor for Ministry* (2014) and *What Clergy*

Do When it Looks Like Nothing (2014) as well as a number of book chapters and journal articles.

Martyn Percy is the Dean of Christ Church, Oxford. From 2004–14 he was the Principal of Ripon College Cuddesdon, one of the largest Anglican ordination training centers in the world. He has also undertaken a number of roles with charities and in public life, including being a Director of the Advertising Standards Authority and an Advisor to the British Board of Film Classification. He writes on religion in contemporary culture and modern ecclesiology. He teaches for the Faculty of Theology and Religion at the University of Oxford, and tutors in the Social Sciences Division and at the Saïd Business School. His publications include *Anglicanism: Confidence, Commitment and Communion* (2013); *The Future Shapes of Anglicanism: Charts, Currents, Contours* (2017); and *The Humble Church: Renewing the Body of Christ* (2021).

Altagracia Pérez-Bullard is the Director of Contextual Ministry and Assistant Professor of Practical Theology at Virginia Theological Seminary in Alexandria, VA. Altagracia has served in ministry over thirty years as youth minister, community leader, and priest in the dioceses of New York, Chicago, and Los Angeles. She was the Canon for Congregational Vitality in the Episcopal Diocese of New York; and Rector of Holy Faith Church, Inglewood, and St. Philip's, in South Los Angeles. She has brought leadership to the issues of HIV/AIDS, youth violence, worker justice and living wage, health disparities in communities of color, housing, and community empowerment. In each of these areas she has sought to build bridges and create alliances between communities across lines of difference, whether they are characterized by race, ethnicity, class, gender, sexuality, or physical and mental abilities.

Sam Portaro is a retired priest of the Episcopal Church. He served as Vicar of the Church of the Epiphany in Newton, NC; Episcopal Chaplain to the College of William & Mary and Associate Rector of Bruton Parish Church in Williamsburg, VA, from 1976 until 1982; and Episcopal Chaplain and Director of Brent House at The University of Chicago, 1982–2004; CREDO Faculty, 2005–17. Author of seven books, numerous essays and articles, he conducts Quiet Days, retreats, and has served as a consultant, educator, and preacher nationwide and in England, and is a Trustee of the Pullman

Educational Foundation in Chicago. He lives in Chicago with his spouse, Christopher Dionesotes, with whom he enjoys cooking, music, theater, movies, reading, and the endless cultural and culinary bounty of that beautiful city.

Christina Rees, CBE, is a writer and commentator, contributing over the past thirty years to many newspapers, journals, and anthologies, and on radio and television. She speaks and preaches both nationally and internationally. She was a leading campaigner for the ordination of women in the Church of England, and chaired Women and the Church (WATCH) for over thirteen years. She was a member of the General Synod for twenty-five years and a founder member of the Archbishops' Council, as well as serving on many national committees. She was on the governing body of Ripon College Cuddesdon, a leading theological college, and serves as a trustee for a number of Christian charities. She is Acting Chair of the Li Tim-Oi Foundation, a grant-making body for women in the Two Thirds world. Christina's books include *The Divine Embrace* (2000); *Voices of this Calling: Experiences of the First Generation of Women Priests* (2002); and *Feast + Fast, Food for Lent and Easter* (2011). She was born on Long Island in the United States and has traveled widely. She now lives in north Norfolk, England, with her husband Chris, where they run a communications consultancy and where Christina is a part-time school chaplain. In 2015 she was made a Commander of the British Empire for services to the Church of England.

Robert Boak Slocum is the author, editor, or co-editor of thirteen books, including *The Anglican Imagination: Portraits and Sketches of Modern Anglican Theologians* (2015); *Light in a Burning-Glass: A Systematic Presentation of Austin Farrer's Theology* (2007); *Seeing & Believing: Reflections for Faith*; and *The Theology of William Porcher DuBose: Life, Movement, and Being* (2000). He taught theology courses at Marquette University on Christ and culture, explorations in Christian theology, and quests for God. He later served at St. Catharine College in Kentucky as Dean of the School of Arts & Sciences and taught courses in religious studies and applied ethics. He was the President of the Society of Anglican and Lutheran Theologians, and Co-Convenor of the Society for the Study of Anglicanism. He served on the board of the Anglian Theological Review. He was the clergy in charge of congregations in the dioceses of Louisiana, Milwaukee, and Lexington.

He was ecumenical officer of the Diocese of Lexington. He currently serves as the Narrative Medicine Program Coordinator at University of Kentucky HealthCare, where he teaches an elective rotation for senior medical students on the narrative basis for patient care and resilient practice. He serves on the Hospital Ethics Committee. He lives in Danville, Kentucky, with his wife, Victoria. He has three grown children, Claire, Rebecca, and Jacob.

Alan Wilson is Bishop of Buckingham. He is Chair of the Oxford Diocesan Board of Education (ODBE), one of the largest in the country, serving over three hundred state schools in the Thames Valley. Until December 2019 he was a founding member of the Oxford Nandyal Education Foundation, a schools' development charity that worked in Andhra Pradesh, India. He has chaired Art Beyond Belief, an Interfaith Education Trust, and Christians Aware, an Interfaith Education Trust based in Leicester, from 2011–14. He is a member of Council at Wycombe Abbey School and Associate Governor of Cressex Community School, a Co-operative Community Trust. He was on the Diocesan Board of Social Responsibility from 2003–09. He served on the Oxford Diocesan Safeguarding Committee from 2003–10. He is a member of the Anglican Peace and Justice Network. He is the author of *More Perfect Union? Understanding Same-Sex Marriage* (2014). When named as a leading straight ally of gay rights in the *Independent* on the Sunday 2014 Rainbow List he was described as one of the most vocal supporters of equal marriage in the Church of England. Arising from extensive work supporting survivors of Abuse in Church 2019, he and his colleague, Chaplain Canon Rosie Harper, co-authored *To Heal and Not to Hurt: A Fresh Approach to Safeguarding in Church* (2019). He was a witness at the Anglican Church hearings of the British Government's Independent Inquiry into Child Sex Abuse.

Bill Wylie-Kellermann is a nonviolent community activist and United Methodist pastor retired from St. Peter's Episcopal Church Detroit. He has authored seven books, among them most recently *Principalities in Particular* (2017), and *Celebrant's Flame: Daniel Berrigan in Memory and Reflection* (2021). He is cofounder of Word and World: A Peoples' School, and adjunct faculty at Ecumenical Theological Seminary, Detroit. A graduate of Union Theological Seminary in New York City, he's been engaged in nonviolent direct action for justice and peace for five decades, most recently with the Detroit water struggle and the Michigan Poor People's Campaign. In Jesus, he bets his life on gospel nonviolence, good news to the poor, Word made flesh, and freedom from the power of death.

Bibliography

Adam, David. *Aiden, Bede, Cuthbert: Three Inspirational Saints*. London: SPCK, 2006.

Aheron, Grace. "Do I Want to Inherit This Theology?" *Geez Magazine* no. 59, Winter 2021.

Appleton, George, ed. *The Oxford Book of Prayer*. Oxford: Oxford University Press, 1985.

The Book of Common Prayer according to the Use of the Episcopal Church. New York: Church Publishing, 1979.

Berger, Peter L. *A Rumor of Angels: Modern Society and the Rediscovery of the Supernatural*. Garden City, NY: Doubleday, 1969.

Betinis, Abbie. "Resilience." https://www.allvoiceschoralproject.org/resilience.php.

"Bill of Mortality from 1665 London." *Pique Show* (blog), December 22, 2016. https://www.piqueshow.com/home/2016/12/22/bill-of-mortality-from-1665-london.

"The Black Report 1980." https://www.sochealth.co.uk/national-health-service/public-health-and-wellbeing/poverty-and-inequality/the-black-report-1980.

"Blair Calls for Lifestyle Change." *BBC News*, July 26, 2006. http://news.bbc.co.uk/1/hi/5215548.stm.

Boff, Clodovis. "Epistemology and Method of the Theology of Liberation." In *Mysteriium Liberationis: Fundamental Concepts of Liberation Theology*, edited by Ignacio Ellacuría and Jon Sobrino, 57–84. Maryknoll, NY: Orbis, 1993.

Bonhoeffer, Dietrich. *The Cost of Discipleship*. Translated by R. H. Fuller, Irmgard Booth. New York: Macmillan, 1959.

Booty, John. "Introduction." In *John Donne: Selections from Divine Poems, Sermons, Devotions, and Prayers*, edited by John Booty, 9–72. New York: Paulist, 1990.

Boyle, David. *Peace on Earth: The Christmas Truce of 1914*. 2nd ed. N.p.: Real, 2016.

Buechner, Frederick. *Wishful Thinking: A Theological ABC*. New York: Harper & Row, 1973.

Camus, Albert. *The Plague*. New York: Knopf, 1948.

Chittister, Joan. "Xenophilia, The Love of Strangers." In *Illuminated Life: Monastic Wisdom for Seekers of Light*, 126–30. Maryknoll, NY: Orbis, 2010.

Daniels, Jonathan. "A Burning Bush, April, 1965." In *American Martyr: The Jon Daniels Story*, edited by William J. Schneider, 69–70. Harrisburg, PA: Morehouse, 1992.

———. "To Mary Elizabeth MacNaughton, Selma, Alabama, March 29, 1965." In *American Martyr: The Jon Daniels Story*, edited by William J. Schneider, 69–70. Harrisburg, PA: Morehouse, 1992.

———. "To Molly D. Thoron, Selma, Alabama, April 15, 1965." In *American Martyr: The Jon Daniels Story*, edited by William J. Schneider, 72–73. Harrisburg, PA: Morehouse, 1992.

de Gruchy, John. *Theology and Ministry in Context and Crisis*. Grand Rapids, MI: Eerdmans, 1987.

Dehqani-Tafti, H. B. *The Hard Awakening*. New York: Seabury, 1981.

———. *The Unfolding Design of My World: A Pilgrim in Exile*. Edited by Kenneth Cragg. Norwich: Canterbury, 2000.

Donne, John. "Devotion XVI." In *John Donne: Selections from Divine Poems, Sermons, Devotions, and Prayers*, edited by John Booty, 267–70. New York: Paulist, 1990.

———. "Devotion XVII." In *John Donne: Selections from Divine Poems, Sermons, Devotions, and Prayers*, edited by John Booty, 271–73. New York: Paulist, 1990.

———. "Station No. 6: The Physician Is Afraid: Expostulation." In *Devotions upon Emergent Occasions and Death's Duel with The Life of Dr. John Donne*, by Izaak Walton, 32–38. New York: Vintage, 1999.

Eagles, Charles W. *Outside Agitator: Jon Daniels and the Civil Rights Movement in Alabama*. Tuscaloosa, AL: University of Alabama, 2000.

"End of Year Stats." https://www.trusselltrust.org/news-and-blog/latest-stats/end-year-stats/.

"The English Indices of Deprivation 2019." https://assets.publishing.service.gov.uk/government/uploads/system/uploads/attachment_data/file/835115/IoD2019_Statistical_Release.pdf.

Farrer, Austin. "The Rational Grounds for Belief in God." In *Austin Farrer, Reflective Faith: Essays in Philosophical Theology*, edited by Charles C. Conti, 7-23. Grand Rapids, MI: Eerdmans, 1973.

Feiler, Bruce. *America's Prophet: Moses and the American Story*. New York: Morrow, 2010.

"Food Banks Report Record Spike in Need as Coalition of Anti-poverty Charities Call for Strong Lifeline to be Thrown to Anyone Who Needs It." https://www.trusselltrust.org/2020/05/01/coalition-call/.

Forest, Jim. *The Root of War Is Fear: Thomas Merton's Advice to Peacemakers*. Maryknoll, NY: Orbis, 2016.

Francis-Devine, Brigid. "Research Briefing: Poverty in the UK: Statistics." https://commonslibrary.parliament.uk/research-briefings/sn07096/.

"Fraud and Error in the Benefit System: Latest Data from DWP for Great Britain in 2020–21." https://femavis.herokuapp.com/index.html.

Goodson, Albert, ed. and comp. *Lift Every Voice and Sing II*. New York: Church Publishing, 1993.

Gosse, Edmund. *The Life and Letters of John Donne, Dean of St. Paul's, Vol. II*. London: Hienemann, 1899.

Graunt, John. *London's Dreadful Visitation, or, A Collection of All the Bills of Mortality for This Present Year Beginning the 20th of December, 1664, and Ending the 19th of December Following: As Also the General or Whole Years Bill (1665)*. London: Cotes, 1665.

Gutiérrez, Gustavo. *A Theology of Liberation: History, Politics and Salvation*. Translated and edited by Sister Caridad Inda and John Eagleson. London: SCM, 1973. https://www.academia.edu/4857489/A_Theology_of_Liberation.

Hanh, Thich Nhat. "Please Call Me By My True Names." In *Call Me By My True Names: The Collected Poems of Thich Nhat Hanh*, 72–73. Berkeley, CA: Parallax, 1999.

Hall, Amy Laura. *Laughing at the Devil: Seeing the World with Julian of Norwich*. Durham: Duke University, 2018.

Hartnell, Jack. *Medieval Bodies: Life, Death and Art in the Middle Ages*. London: Profile, 2018.

Hatcher, John. *The Black Death: A Personal History*. Cambridge: Da Capo, 2008.

Hood, Andrew, and Tom Waters. "The Impact of Tax and Benefit Reforms on Household Incomes." https://www.ifs.org.uk/publications/9164.

"Hungry for Change: Fixing the Failures in Food." https://committees.parliament.uk/publications/1762/documents/17092/default/.

Julian of Norwich. *Showings*. Translated by Edmund Colledge and James Walsh. New York: Paulist, 1978.

Justice Choir. "24. Resilience (by Abbie Betinis), perf. UNF Chamber Singers." *YouTube*, January 21, 2018. https://www.youtube.com/watch?v=jB6c6aOGEGY.

Kendi, Ibram X. *How to Be an Antiracist*. New York: One World, 2019.

Kirk-Duggan, Cheryl A. *Exorcising Evil: A Womanist Perspective on the Spirituals*. Maryknoll, NY: Orbis, 1997.

Kisner, Jordan. *Thin Places: Essays from In Between*. New York: Farrar, Straus & Giroux, 2020.

Kübler-Ross, Elisabeth. *On Death and Dying*. New York: Macmillan, 1969.

Kushner, Harold. *When Bad Things Happen to Good People*. New York: Schocken, 1978.

Lamott, Anne. *Operating Instructions: A Journal of My Son's First Year*. New York: Anchor, 2005.

———. *Traveling Mercies: Some Thoughts on Faith*. New York: Anchor, 1999.

Lander, Clara. "Per Fretum Febris, Through the Straits of Fever: A Study of the Relationship between Theme and Form in John Donne's Devotions Upon Emergent Occasions, and Severall Steps in my Sickness." PhD diss., University of Manitoba, 1968.

Lewis, C. S. *The Silver Chair*. London: Bles, 1953.

Lynch, Thomas. "Good Grief." *Christian Century*, July 26, 2003.

———. *The Undertaking: Life Studies from the Dismal Trade*. New York: Penguin, 1998.

Macmurray, John. *Persons in Relation (The Form of the Personal)*. London: Faber & Faber, 1970.

Marmot, Michael, et al. "Contribution of Job Control and Other Risk Factors to Social Variations of Coronary Heart Disease Incidence." *Lancet* 350.9073 (1997) 235–39.

Marmot, Michael, et al. "Health Equity in England: The Marmot Review 10 Years On." https://www.health.org.uk/publications/reports/the-marmot-review-10-years-on.

McEnroe, Colin. "On Solitude and Hermits." *The Colin McEnroe Show*, April 15, 2020. https://omny.fm/shows/the-colin-mcenroe-show/on-solitude-and-hermits.

McGinn, Bernard. *The Harvest of Christian Mysticism in Medieval Germany*. New York: Crossroad, 2005.

Menakem, Resmaa. *My Grandmother's Hands*. Las Vegas, NV: Central Recovery, 2017.

Mortimer, Ian. *The Time Traveller's Guide to Elizabethan England*. London: Bodley Head, 2012.

Murphy, Jim. *Truce: The Day the Soldiers Stopped Fighting*. New York: Scholastic, 2009.

Nuth, Joan M. *God's Lovers in an Age of Anxiety: The Medieval English Mystics*. London: Darton, Longman & Todd, 2001.

———. *Wisdom's Daughter: The Theology of Julian of Norwich*. Spring Valley, NY: Crossroad, 1991.

O'Connor, Patricia. *In Search of Thérèse*. Vol. 3 of *The Way of the Christian Mystics*. Noel Dermot O'Donoghue. Wilmington, DE: Glazier, 1987.

The Order of Saint Helena. *The Saint Helena Breviary*, Personal Edition. New York: Church Publishing, 2019.

Perez, Caroline Criado. *Invisible Women: Exposing Data Bias in a World Designed for Men*. London: Random House, 2019.

Phillips, Adam, and Barbara Taylor. *On Kindness*. London: Penguin, 2010.

Phillips, David, and Polly Simpson. "Changes in Councils' Adult Social Care and Overall Service Spending in England, 2009–10 to 2017–18." https://www.ifs.org.uk/ publications/13066.

"Poverty in the UK." https://researchbriefings.files.parliament.uk/documents/SN07096/ SN07096.pdf.

Public Health England. "Disparities in the Risk and Outcomes of COVID-19." https://assets.publishing.service.gov.uk/government/uploads/system/uploads/ attachment_data/file/908434/Disparities_in_the_risk_and_outcomes_of_COVID_ August_2020_update.pdf.

Report of the Archbishop of Canterbury's Commission on Urban Priority Areas. *Faith in the City: A Call for Action by Church and Nation*. London: Church House Publishing, 1985.

Robb, Farifteh. *In the Shadow of the Shahs: Finding Unexpected Grace*. Oxford: Lion, 2020.

Rose, Jacqueline. "Pointing the Finger: Jacqueline Rose on The Plague." *The London Review of Books*, May 7, 2020. https://lrb.co.uk/the-paper/v42/n09/jacqueline-rose/ pointing-the-finger.

Roy, Arundhati. "The Pandemic Is a Portal." *Financial Times*, April 3, 2020. https://www. ft.com/content/10d8f5e8-74eb-11ea-95fe-fcd274e920ca.

Schmidt, Joseph F. *Everything Is Grace: The Life and Way of Thérèse of Lisieux*. Ijamsville, MD: The Word Among Us, 2007.

Schneider, William J. *American Martyr: The Jon Daniels Story*. Harrisburg, PA: Morehouse, 1992.

Schrecker, Ted, and Clare Bambra. *How Politics Makes Us Sick: Neoliberal Epidemics*. Basingstoke: Palgrave Macmillan, 2015.

Scott, Courtney, et al. "Affordability of the UK's Eatwell Guide." https://foodfoundation. org.uk/publication/affordability-uks-eatwell-guide.

Slocum, Robert Boak. "Christmas Trees and Chocolate Cake." In *Seeing & Believing: Reflections for Faith, A Devotional Journal*, edited by Robert Boak Slocum, np. Eugene, OR: Wipf & Stock, 2019.

———. "Jonathan Daniels: Faith, Freedom, and Sacrifice." *Anglican and Episcopal History* 89.2 (2020) 1–14.

———. *Light in a Burning-Glass: A Systematic Presentation of Austin Farrer's Theology*. Eugene, OR: Wipf & Stock, 2019.

Snowden, Frank M. *Epidemics and Society: From the Black Death to the Present*. New Haven: Yale, 2019.

Sobrino, Jon. "The Central Position of the Reign of God in Liberation Theology." In *An Eerdmans Reader in Contemporary Political Theology*, edited by William T. Cavanaugh et al., 194–216. Grand Rapids, MI: Eerdmans, 2012.

"Socio-economic Inequalities in Avoidable Mortality, England and Wales 2001–17." https://www.ons.gov.uk/peoplepopulationandcommunity/healthandsocialcare/

causesofdeath/articles/measuringsocioeconomicinequalities
inavoidablemortalityinenglandandwales2001to2017.

Stringfellow, William. "Care Enough to Weep." *The Witness*, December 21, 1963.

———. *An Ethic for Christians and Other Aliens in a Strange Land*. Waco, TX: Word, 1973.

———. *Free in Obedience*. New York: Seabury, 1964.

———. *My People Is the Enemy: An Autobiographical Polemic*. Eugene, OR: Wipf & Stock, 2005.

Stuckler, David, and Sanju Basu. *The Body Economic: Why Austerity Kills*. New York: Basic, 2013.

Thérèse of Lisieux. *Story of a Soul: The Autobiography of St. Thérèse of Lisieux*. 2nd ed. Translated by John Clark. Washington, DC: ICS, 1976.

Thomas, R. S. *A Choice of George Herbert's Verse*. London: Faber & Faber, 1967.

Ting, K. H. "A Chinese Example: The Silences of the Bible." In *Voices from the Margin: Interpreting the Bible in the Third World*, edited by R. S. Sugirtharajah, 431–33. Maryknoll, NY: Orbis, 2006.

Tuchmann, Barbara W. *A Distant Mirror: The Calamitous Fourteenth Century*. New York: Knopf, 1979.

United Nations General Assembly. *Universal Declaration of Human Rights*. https://www.un.org/en/about-us/universal-declaration-of-human-rights.

Walton, Izaac. "The Life and Death of Dr Donne, Late Deane of St Pauls London." In *Poetry & Prose: With Izaac Walton's Life*, by John Donne, xvii–xliv. Oxford: Clarendon, 1946.

Walzer, Michael. *Exodus and Revolution*. New York: Basic, 1985.

Weintraub, Stanley. *Silent Night*. New York: Penguin, 2001.

Welby, Justin. *Reimagining Britain: Foundations for Hope*. London: Bloomsbury Continuum, 2018.

Welch, Sharon D. *A Feminist Ethic of Risk*. Rev. ed. Minneapolis: Fortress, 2000.

White, Chris, and Asim Butt. "Inequality in Health and Life Expectancies within Upper Tier Local Authorities: 2009 to 2013." https://www.ons.gov.uk/people populationandcommunity/healthandsocialcare/healthandlifeexpectancies /bulletins/inequalityinhealthandlifeexpectancieswithinuppertierlocal authorities/2009to2013.

Whyte, David. *Consolations, Nourishment and Underlying Meaning of Everyday Words*. Langley, WA: Many Rivers, 2016.

Wilkinson, Richard, and Kate Pickett. *The Spirit Level: Why Equality Is Better for Everyone*. New York: Penguin, 2010.

Wills, Garry. *Head and Heart: American Christianities*. New York: Penguin, 2007.

Wink, Walter. *Engaging the Powers*. Minneapolis: Fortress, 1992.

———. *Naming the Powers*. Philadelphia: Fortress, 1984.

———. *Unmasking the Powers*. Philadelphia: Fortress, 1986.

Wright, N. T. *Surprised by Hope*. London: SPCK, 2011.

Wylie-Kellermann, Bill. "Not Against Flesh and Blood." *Geez Magazine* no. 59, Winter 2021.

———. *Principalities in Particular: A Practical Theology of the Powers*. Minneapolis: Fortress, 2017.

———. "Prayer for Mr. Trump, the Human Being." *Radical Discipleship*, October 4, 2020. https://radicaldiscipleship.net/2020/10/04/prayer-for-mr-trump-the-human-being/.

Milton Keynes UK
Ingram Content Group UK Ltd.
UKHW021926220124
436492UK00013B/1096